Logic Gates

Ahoy, curious companions.
Do you have a smartphone or tablet video games or watch television? D(do you have a digital watch? All the gadgets would not exist without Logic Gates in them.

But what are Logic Gates?
Now, these Logic Gates are like little decision-makers. They have rules they follow to decide what to do with the information they get. Logic Gates are like the wizards behind the scenes making sure everything works just right. Standard personal computers typically have several millions to a few billions Logic Gates.

In the following pages, we embark on a journey through the wonders of the Logic Gates. Fun and learning will go hand-in-hand when we solve easy and difficult puzzles.

Together, we will navigate through 43 challenges that will test your knowledge and creativity. Put on your thinking caps, and let's set sail on an adventure like no other, brave minds!

In this book, we learn about:
The AND Gate, NAND Gate, OR Gate, XOR Gate, NOR Gate, XNOR Gate, NOT Gate, Buffer, IMPLY Gate, NIMPLY Gate, Tristate Buffer, Mux, Demux, Half Adder, Full Adder, Set-Reset Latch, Gated Set-Reset Latch, D Latch, Boolean Truth Tables, Universal Logic Gates, and Binary Addition.

Solutions are added at the end of the book... Can you do it without?

Content Table

1. Meet Andy, Olly, and Nellie.. 5
2. A Party with our 3 New Friends.. 11
3. Meet the Family of our 3 Friends.. 17
4. Some More Family.. 23
5. Exclusive Superheroes.. 27
6. Universal Logic Gates... 37
7. Some Strange Creatures... 53
8. The Snakes are coming... 67
9. Something more difficult to end... 75
Solutions.. 81

1. Meet Andy, Olly, and Nellie

Within electronic devices and gadgets, you will always find three friendly characters: **Andy** the AND Gate, **Olly** the OR Gate, and **Nellie** the NOT Gate.
Let's get to know them!

Andy the AND Gate:
Andy is a gate who's all about both things happening together. So, if you ask Andy, "Should we go to the park?" He'll only say "Yes" if both the weather is sunny AND we have ice cream. If one of these things is missing, Andy says "No".

To get to know Andy better, we can describe his behavior in a table. We call this Andy's **Truth Table**, as it gives an overview of his answer depending on the situation:

Is the weather sunny?	Will we have ice cream?	Andy's Answer
Yes	No	No
Yes	Yes	Yes
No	No	No
No	Yes	No

As Andy wants things to happen together, he will only answer "Yes" when the weather is sunny AND we will have ice cream! If we replace "Yes" by 1, and "No" by 0, the Truth Table becomes a **Boolean Truth Table**, which is a way smart people describe the behavior of Andy, but it just tells the same thing as our table above. We can replace the question above the first column with "A", the question above the second column with "B", and Andy's answer with "Q", the table then becomes:

A	B	Q
1	0	0
1	1	1
0	0	0
0	1	0

Some even smarter people will describe Andy's behavior in a more difficult way, with a crazy symbol on top of the table:

		A	
		0	1
B	0	0	0
	1	0	1

If you look very good, you see that this table just tells the same thing as the previous tables above, with the answer of Andy (Q) being only equal to "Yes" (1) when it is both sunny (A = 1) and we will have ice cream (B = 1). The crazy symbol used by smart people has the letters A and B on the left, as these are the questions that are asked at Andy. They are the inputs that Andy will need to come up with an answer. The letter Q is on the right, representing the answer Andy gives. Try to remember this symbol, as we will see it again further on.
Now that you know Andy, can you fill in his behavior?:

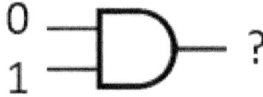

Q 1

Easy-peasy, right?! Now let's meet Andy's friend, Olly.

Olly the OR Gate:

Olly is a gate that's more easygoing. He says "Yes" as long as one of the things is OK. So, if you ask Olly, "Should we go to the park?" He'll say "Yes" if either it's a sunny day OR we have ice cream. Even if just one of these things is true, Olly is up for it!

As you know, we can get to know Olly better, by looking at his **Truth Table**:

Is the weather sunny?	Will we have ice cream?	Olly's Answer
Yes	No	Yes
Yes	Yes	Yes
No	No	No
No	Yes	Yes

As Olly is more easygoing than Andy, he will answer three times "Yes", each time only one thing has to be true. Olly is happy with at least one thing. What a great friend to hang around with!

The **Boolean Truth Table** of Olly becomes somewhat different compared with Andy's table we saw above. You should be able to create this table yourself by now:

A	B	Q
1	0	?
1	1	?
0	0	?
0	1	?

Q 2

Again, a piece of cake, right?!

Similar as Andy's behavior, we can use a symbol to describe Olly's. Try to also remember this symbol, as we will need it again further on:

		A	A
		0	1
B	0	0	1
	1	1	1

You already know this, but let's repeat it one more time: The letters A and B are the questions that are asked at Olly. They are the inputs he will need to come up with an answer. The letter Q represents the answer Olly gives. The answer of Olly (Q) will be equal to "Yes" (1) when it is sunny (A = 1) OR we will have ice cream (B = 1).

So far, we got to know Andy and Olly. Can you fill in their behavior?:

Q 3

You noticed the difference between Andy and Olly?

Now let's meet the final one of our three friendly characters: Nellie the NOT Gate.

Nellie the NOT Gate:

Nellie is a gate with a bit of a twist. She likes to tell the opposite of what's going on. So, if you ask Nellie, "Is it raining?" She'll say "No" when it's raining and "Yes" when it is not. She likes to switch things around!

As Nellie likes to turn things upside down, we sometimes call her an **Inverter**. She outputs the opposite of the input she gets. Her **Truth Table** looks very simple, she just answers the opposite of the question asked:

Is it raining?	Nellie's Answer
Yes	No
No	Yes

Nellie's **Boolean Truth Table**—with another new symbol in it—looks very easy now, as we only have one input. The little circle on the symbol is called a **Bubble**, indicating that Nellie turns things upside down between the input (A) and the output (Q).

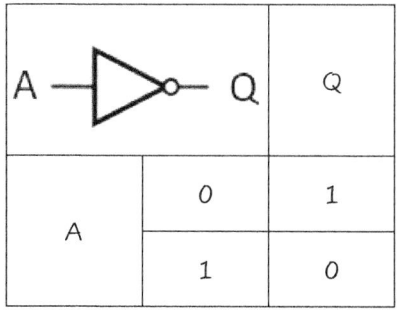

This is simple, right?! No need to make an exercise about Nellie's behavior.

2. A Party with our 3 New Friends

We just started our adventure and we already made three new friends: **Andy** the AND Gate, **Olly** the OR Gate, and **Nellie** the NOT Gate. We learned how **Truth Tables** and **Boolean Truth Tables** can be used to describe the behavior of our new friends. We also learned three different symbols as a picture of each of our friends. You remember them, right?! Let's list them up one more time:

Andy	AND Gate	A ─⊐D─ Q B
Olly	OR Gate	A ─⊐D─ Q B
Nellie	NOT Gate	A ─▷o─ Q

Until now, we only asked questions to each of our new friends by themselves. Why not have a party with all our new friends together. We can ask questions to one another, so we all get to know each other.

We can ask Andy the question (A) "Is the weather sunny?" and (B) "Will we have ice cream?" We ask Nellie (C) "Is it raining?" We ask Olly "Should we go to the park?" and Olly will use the answers of Andy and Nellie to come up with an answer himself (Q). We can use the symbols we learned to present what's going on:

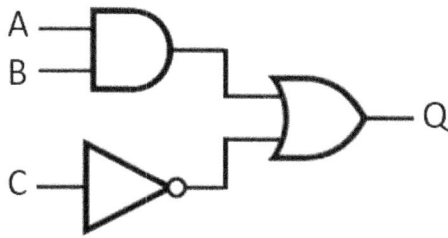

Can you imagine how the **Boolean Truth Table** will look like to describe the behavior of our three friends together? Let's try to do this together!

We know the behavior of Andy, Olly, and Nellie by themselves. So, when they meet each other at a party, they will behave in a similar way.

We learned that Andy wants things to happen together. The answer of Andy will only equal "Yes" (1) when it is both sunny (A = 1) and we will have ice cream (B = 1).

Nellie outputs the opposite of the input she gets. The answer of Nellie will equal "Yes" (1) when it is not raining (C = 0) and she will answer "No" (0) when it is raining (C = 1).

Olly is more easygoing. He says "Yes" as long as one of the things is OK. As Olly uses the answers of Andy and Nellie to come up with an answer himself, he will answer "Yes" (1) as long as Andy or Nellie come up with "Yes" (1) as an answer.

Try to understand the way the **Boolean Truth Table** is created as it will be important for the next part of our journey. (If you don't immediately see how it works, look at the little tip and trick on the next page!)

		AB			
		00	01	10	11
C	0	0	1	1	1
	1	1	0	0	0	1

Tip: A little trick to create a more complex **Boolean Truth Table** is to fill in each cell step-by-step. Start with the outcome of Andy and write this in each cell in the table. You will only get a 1 in the last column as Andy only answers "Yes" when both inputs (A & B) are true:

	AB			
	00	01	10	11
C 0	0	0	0	1
C 1	0	0	0	1

Now we add the outcome of Nellie in each cell. This is easy as Nellie will just answer the opposite of the input (C). So, 0 becomes 1, and 1 becomes 0:

	AB			
	00	01	10	11
C 0	01	01	01	11
C 1	00	00	00	10

To finally find Olly's answers, we use the numbers in each cell as the input for Olly. He will answer "Yes" (1) as long as Andy or Nellie come up with "Yes" (1) as an answer. So, if there is a 1 in a cell, Olly will also give 1 as answer:

		AB			
		00	01	10	11
C	0	0	1	1	1	1
	1	1	0	0	0	1

Now it's your turn!
Assume we ask Olly the question (A) "Is the weather sunny?" and (B) "Will we have ice cream?" We ask Nellie (C) "Is it raining?" We ask Andy "Should we go to the park?" and Andy will use the answers of Olly and Nellie to come up with an answer himself (Q).

The symbols below present what's going on. But how will the **Boolean Truth Table** look like for this situation? Can you fill in the table correctly?

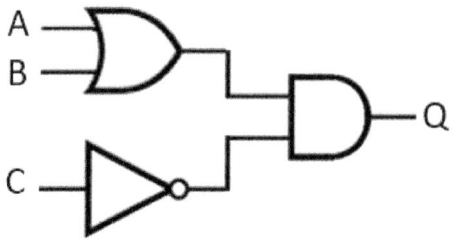

		AB			
		00	01	10	11
C	0				
	1				

Q 4

Can you solve it in one step? You can use the little trick we learned to fill in the table step by step.

How many times do we get 1 as result? Compare this with the number of ones we ended up in the previous table in which Olly gave the final answer. Do you understand where this difference is coming from? As Olly is more easygoing, he will give more ones as outcome compared with Andy. Andy wants things to happen together, making him less likely to give 1 as outcome.

3. Meet the Family of our 3 Friends

So far, we got to know our 3 friends very well. We know how Andy the AND Gate, Olly the OR Gate, and Nellie the NOT Gate behave by themselves. We also learned how they behave when they all party together. Now it's time to meet some family members of Andy, Olly, and Nellie.

Andy has a twin siter called **Andrea**. Olly has a twin brother called **Olliver**. Nellie doesn't have a twin, but a normal brother called **Nelson**.

As Andy and Andrea are twins, they will behave in a similar way. Just like Andy, Andrea is a gate who's all about both things happening together.

In a similar way, Olly and his twin brother Olliver are both more easygoing. Even if just one of two things is true, Olly and Olliver are up for it!

The brother of Nellie is not a twin brother. Nelson will behave somewhat different compared with Nellie. You remember that Nellie likes to turn things upside down. She outputs the opposite of the input she gets. Nelson doesn't like to turn things upside down. We sometimes call Nelson a **Buffer**. His **Truth Table** looks very simple, he will just output the same as the input he gets:

Is it raining?	Nelson's Answer
Yes	Yes
No	No

Nelson's **Boolean Truth Table**—with another new symbol in it—looks very easy now. Remark that the **Bubble** is gone, indicating that Nelson will not turn things upside down between the input (A) and the output (Q):

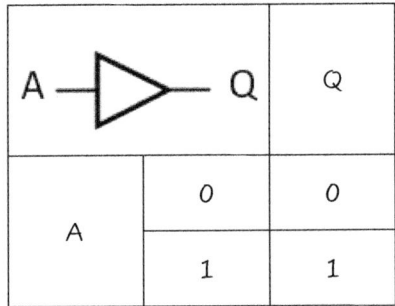

Let's list up everyone we know so far:

Andy & Andrea	AND Gate	A, B → Q
Olly & Olliver	OR Gate	A, B → Q
Nellie	NOT Gate	A → Q
Nelson	Buffer	A → Q

Now we can ask questions to one another, so we all get to know each other. Can you solve all the following riddles correctly?

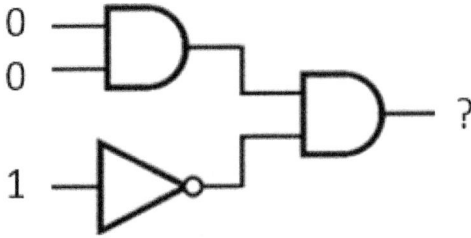

Q 5

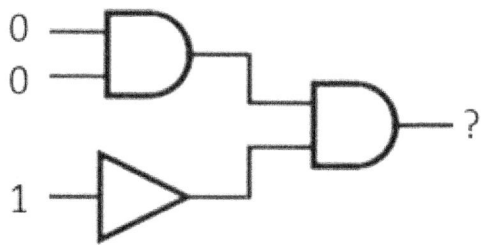

Q 6

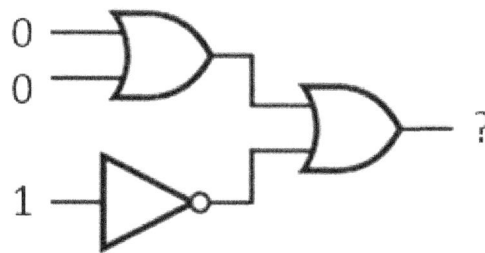

Q 7

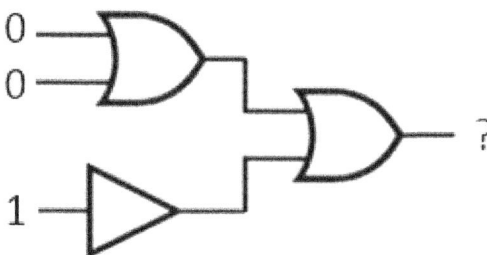

Q 8

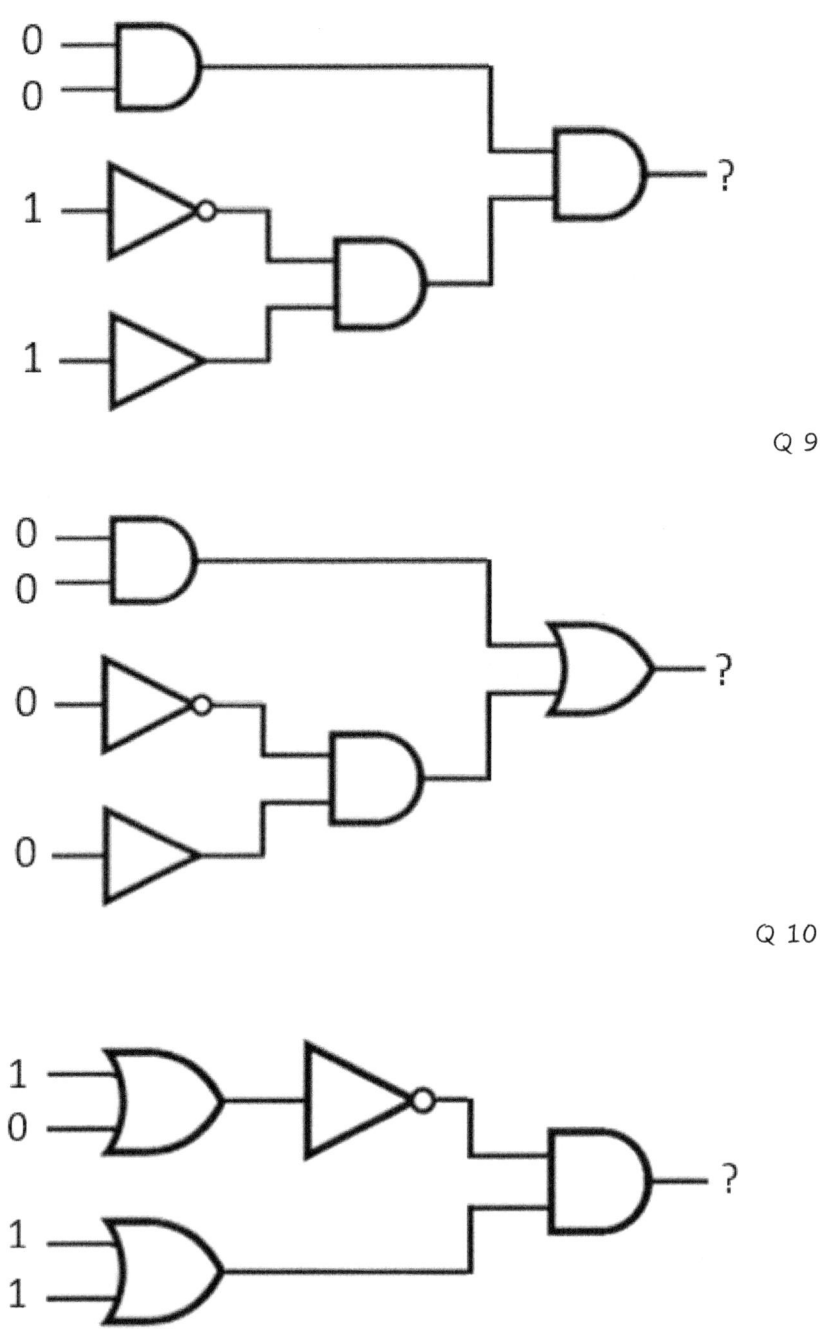

Q 9

Q 10

Q 11

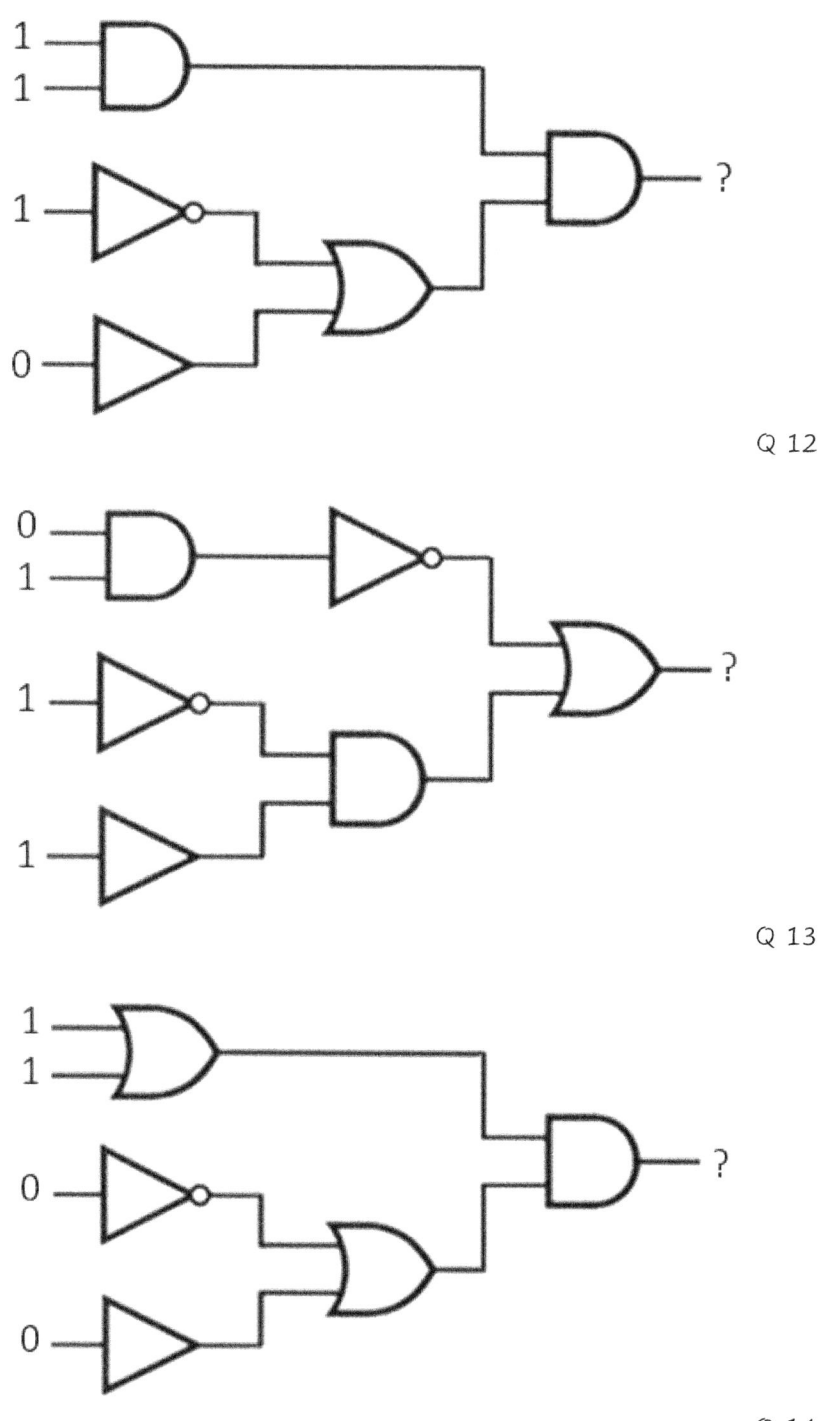

Q 12

Q 13

Q 14

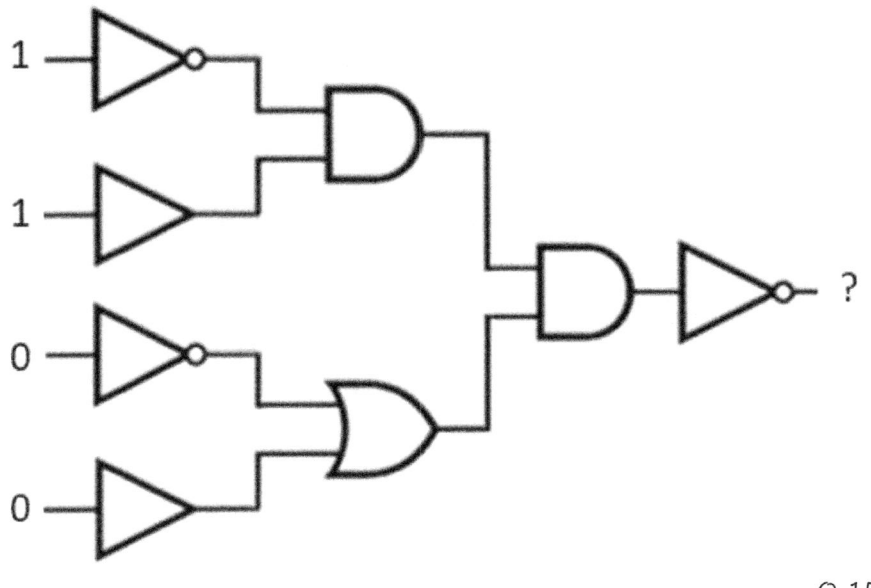

Q 15

4. Some More Family

There are some more family members that we must get to know to fully understand the magical world of the Logic Gates. Let's start with meeting **Nancy** the NAND Gate, and **Nora** the NOR Gate.

Nancy the NAND Gate:
Nancy is a gate who will output the opposite of what Andy the AND Gate will give as outcome. Nancy is a NAND Gate, which stands for a NOT-AND Gate. You remember that Andy is all about both things happening together. Andy will only answer "Yes" when both inputs are true. Nancy, however, will only be happy when things don't happen together. As a result, she will answer "Yes" when no or only one input is true. When both inputs are true, she will answer "No".

Looking at the **Boolean Truth Table** of Nancy, we can immediately see how Nancy always tells the opposite of what Andy is saying:

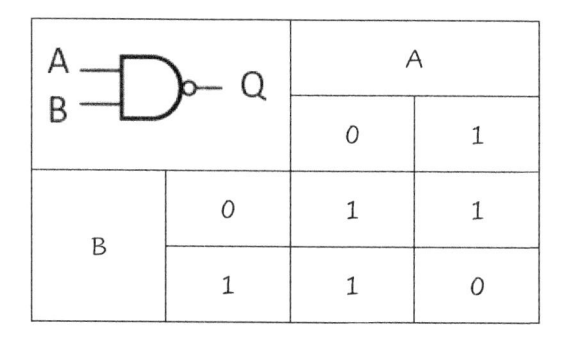

		A	A
		0	1
B	0	1	1
	1	1	0

Compare this table with Andy's table we've seen before. When Andy answers "Yes" (1), Nancy will now answer "No" (0). When Andy answers "No" (0), Nancy will now answer "Yes" (1). The symbol in the table is somewhat similar to the symbol we used for Andy. The only difference is that a **Bubble** is added. Remember that we saw the Bubble appearing when we met Nellie, indicating that Nellie turns things upside down. Here,

the symbol has the same meaning: Nancy acts the same as Andy but will turn everything upside down. Nancy will output the opposite of what Andy will give as outcome.
Can you fill in the behavior of Andy and Nancy?:

$$0 \rightarrow D - ? \quad 0 \rightarrow D\!\circ - ?$$
$$1 \qquad\qquad 1$$

Q 16

Again easy-peasy, right?! Now let's meet Nora.

Nora the NOR Gate:
Nora is a gate who will output the opposite of what Olly the OR Gate will give as outcome. Nora is a NOR Gate, which stands for a NOT-OR Gate. You remember that Olly is a gate that's more easygoing. He says "Yes" as long as one of the things is OK. Nora, however, will only be happy when none of the inputs is true. As a result, she will answer "Yes" when no input is true. She will answer "No" as long as one of the inputs is true.

Looking at the **Boolean Truth Table** of Nora, we can immediately see how Nora always tells the opposite of what Olly is saying:

		A	A
		0	1
B	0	1	0
	1	0	0

Compare this table with Olly's table we've seen before. When Olly answers "Yes" (1), Nora will now answer "No" (0). When

Olly answers "No" (0), Nora will now answer "Yes" (1). The symbol in the table is somewhat similar to the symbol we used for Olly. The only difference is that a **Bubble** is added. This means that Nora acts the same as Olly but will turn everything upside down. Nora will output the opposite of what Olly will give as outcome. Can you fill in the behavior of Olly and Nora?:

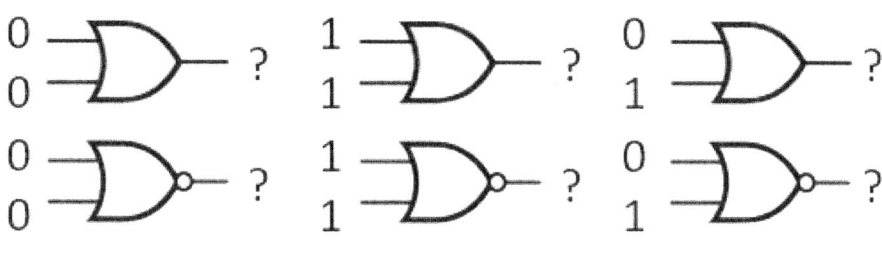

Q 17

OK, this was not so difficult, right?!
Let's repeat again what we learned so far. Do you still remember what each gate is doing?

Andy & Andrea	AND Gate	A, B → Q
Nancy	NAND Gate	A, B → Q
Olly & Olliver	OR Gate	A, B → Q
Nora	NOR Gate	A, B → Q
Nellie	NOT Gate	A → Q
Nelson	Buffer	A → Q

5. Exclusive Superheroes

We learned about Olly the OR Gate and Nora the NOR Gate. On some occasions, these two characters can become superheroes. We then call them X-Gates. Let's learn how that works!

You remember that Olly is a gate that's more easygoing. He says "Yes" as long as one of the things is OK. We look at the **Boolean Truth Table** of Olly again:

		A	
		0	1
B	0	0	1
	1	1	1

Olly is happy with at least one thing. Even if just one of the inputs is true, Olly is up for it!

When we make a superhero of Olly, he becomes an **XOR Gate**. The letters XOR stand for **Exclusive OR**. When being a superhero, Olly will say "Yes" if one, and only one, of the inputs is true. You can see how the **Boolean Truth Table** becomes slightly different with 0 instead of 1 in the lower right corner:

		A	
		0	1
B	0	0	1
	1	1	0

You can see that the output will only be 1 when the two inputs are not equal to each other. When the inputs are equal, the output will be 0. The symbol in the table is somewhat similar to that of the OR Gate. The double line at the left indicates the exclusive functionality of the gate.

What happens when Nora gets superpowers?
You remember that Nora is a gate who will output the opposite of what Olly the OR Gate will give as outcome. When we make a superhero of Nora, she becomes an **XNOR Gate**. The letters XNOR stand for **Exclusive NOT-OR**. When being a superhero, Nora will output the opposite of what Olly the superhero will answer. In other words, the XNOR Gate will give the opposite of what the XOR Gate will give.

Looking at the **Boolean Truth Table** of Nora having superpowers, we see that the output will only be 1 when the two inputs are equal to each other. When the inputs are not equal, the output will be 0. The symbol in the table is somewhat similar to that of the NOR Gate. The double line at the left indicates the exclusive functionality of the gate.

		A	
		0	1
B	0	1	0
	1	0	1

Let's practice this so you learn to understand the logic!
What we learned so far:

Andy & Andrea	AND Gate	A, B → Q
Nancy	NAND Gate	A, B → Q
Olly & Olliver	OR Gate	A, B → Q
Superhero	XOR Gate	A, B → Q
Nora	NOR Gate	A, B → Q
Superhero	XNOR Gate	A, B → Q
Nellie	NOT Gate	A → Q
Nelson	Buffer	A → Q

Can you fill in the following **Boolean Truth Tables** correctly? Think about the little trick we learned to create complex tables!

		AB			
		00	01	10	11
CD	00				
	01				
	10				
	11				

Q 18

		AB			
		00	01	10	11
CD	00				
	01				
	10				
	11				

Q 19

A B C D — (OR, XOR) → AND — ?	AB			
	00	01	10	11
CD 00				
01				
10				
11				

Q 20

A B C D — (OR, AND) → NAND — ?	AB			
	00	01	10	11
CD 00				
01				
10				
11				

Q 21

	AB			
	00	01	10	11
CD 00				
CD 01				
CD 10				
CD 11				

Q 22

	AB			
	00	01	10	11
CD 00				
CD 01				
CD 10				
CD 11				

Q 23

	AB			
	00	01	10	11
CD 00				
CD 01				
CD 10				
CD 11				

Q 24

	AB			
	00	01	10	11
CD 00				
CD 01				
CD 10				
CD 11				

Q 25

	AB			
CD	00	01	10	11
00				
01				
10				
11				

Q 26

	AB			
CD	00	01	10	11
00				
01				
10				
11				

Q 27

		AB			
		00	01	10	11
CD	00				
	01				
	10				
	11				

Q 28

		AB			
		00	01	10	11
CD	00				
	01				
	10				
	11				

Q 29

		AB			
		00	01	10	11
CD	00				
	01				
	10				
	11				

Q 30

6. Universal Logic Gates

We learned about Nancy the NAND Gate and Nora the NOR Gate. Some very smart people discovered that by only asking questions to Nancy the NAND Gate, we are able to get the same behavior of all the other Logic Gates we got to know! The same holds for Nora the NOR Gate: By only asking questions to Nora the NOR Gate, we are able to get the same behavior of all the other Logic Gates we got to know! This is why Nancy the NAND Gate and Nora the NOR Gate are also called **Universal Logic Gates**!

Let's try to understand how this works!

Nancy the NAND Gate as a Universal Logic Gate:
1) Andy and Andrea the AND Gates
We met Andy and Andrea the AND Gates as gates that like things to happen together. These gates will only answer "Yes" (1) when both inputs are true. Let's have a look again at the **Boolean Truth Table** of the AND Gate:

		A	
		0	1
B	0	0	0
	1	0	1

We are able to get a similar **Boolean Truth Table** by only asking questions to Nancy the NAND Gate. We can do this in the following way:

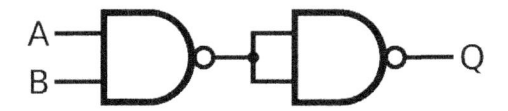

The inputs A and B are given to a first NAND Gate, which gives an output. This output is used for the two inputs of the second NAND Gate, which gives the final output Q.

Let's see if we really get a similar **Boolean Truth Table** by only asking questions to Nancy the NAND Gate. The first NAND Gate will only give 0 as output when both A and B are equal to 1. The second NAND Gate only answers 1 when she gets two 0's as input, which is the result of both A and B being equal to 1. You see that the result is similar to the behavior of an AND Gate. By using only NAND Gates, we were able to reproduce the behavior of the AND Gate. That's why we call the NAND Gate a **Universal Logic Gate**.

A	B	Output 1st NAND Gate	Input 2nd NAND Gate	Q
0	0	1	11	0
0	1	1	11	0
1	0	1	11	0
1	1	0	00	1

2) Olly and Olliver the OR Gates

We met Olly and Olliver the OR Gates as gates that were more easygoing. These gates will answer "Yes" as long as one of the things is OK. Let's have a look again at the **Boolean Truth Table** of the OR Gate:

		A	
		0	1
B	0	0	1
	1	1	1

We are again able to get a similar **Boolean Truth Table** by only asking questions to Nancy the NAND Gate. We can do this in the following way:

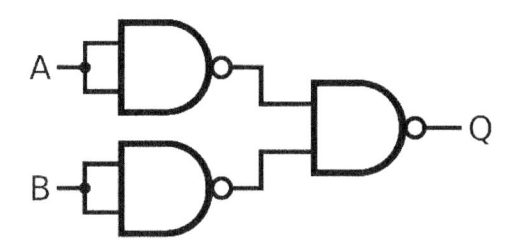

The input A is first used as the two inputs of a first NAND Gate. The input B is used as the two inputs of a second NAND Gate. The output of the first and second NAND Gate will act as the inputs of a third NAND GATE, which gives the final output Q.

Let's again see if we really get a similar **Boolean Truth Table** by only asking questions to Nancy the NAND Gate. The first NAND Gate will only give 1 as output when A is equal to 0. The second NAND Gate acts similar and only answers 1 when B is equal to 0. The third NAND Gate only answers 0 when the input is 11, which is the result of both A and B being equal to 0. You see that the result is similar to the behavior of an OR Gate. By using only NAND Gates, we were able to reproduce the behavior of the OR Gate.

A	Input 1st NAND Gate	Output 1st NAND Gate	B	Input 2nd NAND Gate	Output 2nd NAND Gate	Input 3rd NAND Gate	Q
0	00	1	0	00	1	11	0
0	00	1	1	11	0	10	1
1	11	0	0	00	1	01	1
1	11	0	1	11	0	00	1

3) Superhero Olly the XOR Gate

By now you should understand how it works. Let's look again at the **Boolean Truth Table** of the XOR Gate:

		A	
		0	1
B	0	0	1
	1	1	0

(A, B → Q via XOR gate)

We are able to reproduce the behavior of the XOR Gate by only using NAND Gates. We can do this in the following way:

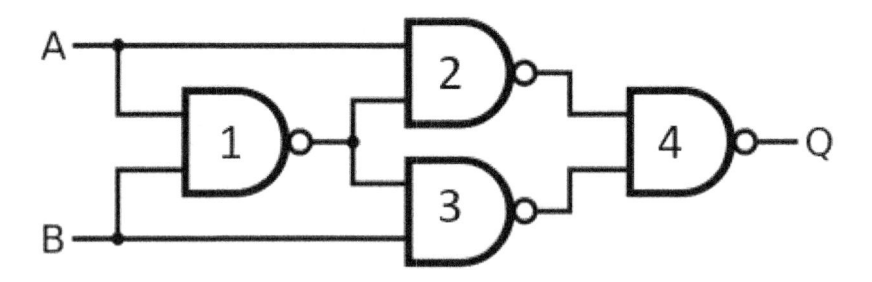

We now have four NAND Gates (we numbered them to get an overview). From the table below you can see that the output is only 1 when only A or only B is equal to 1. This result is similar to the behavior of an XOR Gate.

A	B	Input 1st NAND Gate	Output 1st NAND Gate	Input 2nd NAND Gate	Output 2nd NAND Gate
0	0	00	1	01	1
0	1	01	1	01	1
1	0	10	1	11	0
1	1	11	0	10	1

Input 3rd NAND Gate	Output 3rd NAND Gate	Input 4th NAND Gate	Q
10	1	11	0
11	0	10	1
10	1	01	1
01	1	11	0

4) Nora the NOR Gate

Let's look again at the **Boolean Truth Table** of the NOR Gate:

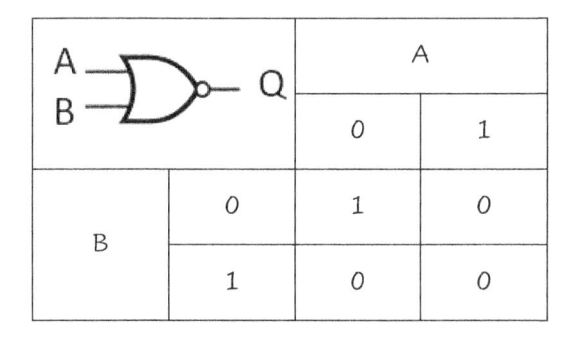

	A=0	A=1
B=0	1	0
B=1	0	0

We are able to reproduce the behavior of the NOR Gate by only using NAND Gates. We can do this in the following way:

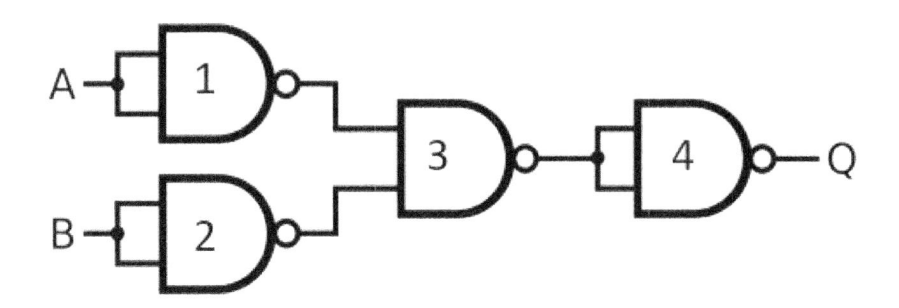

We again have four NAND Gates. From the table below you can see that the output is only 1 when A and B are equal to 0. This result is similar to the behavior of an NOR Gate.

A	Input 1st NAND Gate	Output 1st NAND Gate	B	Input 2nd NAND Gate	Output 2nd NAND Gate
0	00	1	0	00	1
0	00	1	1	11	0
1	11	0	0	00	1
1	11	0	1	11	0

Input 3rd NAND Gate	Output 3rd NAND Gate	Input 4th NAND Gate	Q
11	0	00	1
10	1	11	0
01	1	11	0
00	1	11	0

5) Superhero Nora the XNOR Gate

Let's look again at the **Boolean Truth Table** of the XNOR Gate:

	A	
	0	1
B 0	1	0
1	0	1

We are able to reproduce the behavior of the XNOR Gate by only using NAND Gates. We can do this in the following way:

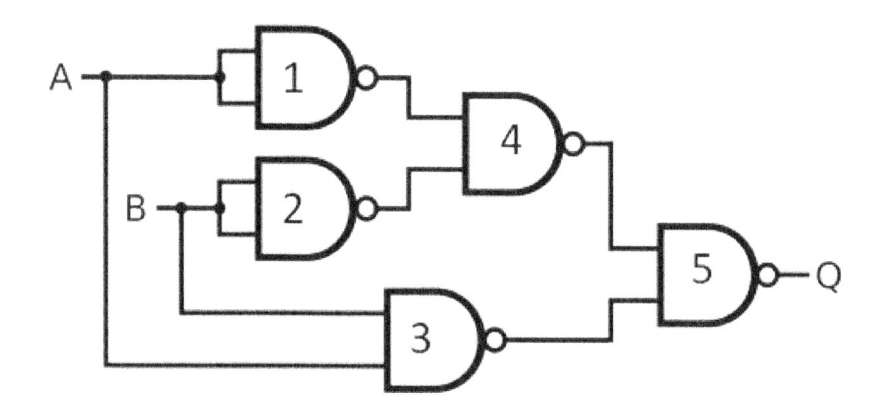

We now have five NAND Gates. From the table below you can see that the output is only 1 when A and B are both equal to 0 or 1. This result is similar to the behavior of an XNOR Gate.

A	Input 1st NAND Gate	Output 1st NAND Gate	B	Input 2nd NAND Gate	Output 2nd NAND Gate
0	00	1	0	00	1
0	00	1	1	11	0
1	11	0	0	00	1
1	11	0	1	11	0

Input 3rd NAND Gate	Output 3rd NAND Gate	Input 4th NAND Gate	Output 4th NAND Gate	Input 5th NAND Gate	Q
00	1	11	0	01	1
10	1	10	1	11	0
01	1	01	1	11	0
11	0	00	1	10	1

43

6) Nellie the NOT Gate

Let's look again at the **Boolean Truth Table** of the NOT Gate:

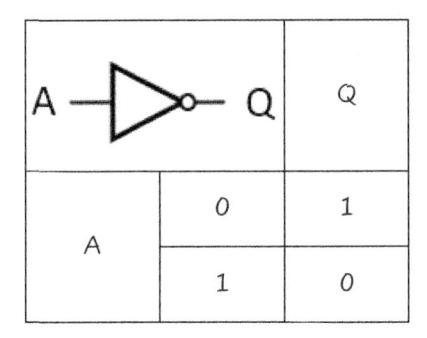

	A	Q
A	0	1
	1	0

We are able to reproduce the behavior of the NOT Gate by only using NAND Gates. We can do this in the following way:

This is easy! The final output will be 1 when A is equal to 0. The output is 0 when A is equal to 1. This result is similar to the behavior of a NOT Gate.

A	Input NAND Gate	Q
0	00	1
1	11	0

Nora the NOR Gate as a Universal Logic Gate:

<u>1) Andy and Andrea the AND Gates</u>

Let's display the **Boolean Truth Table** of the AND Gate again, so we can easily compare it with the result of the NOR Gates:

		A	
		0	1
B	0	0	0
	1	0	1

We are able to get a similar **Boolean Truth Table** by only asking questions to Nora the NOR Gate. We can do this in the following way:

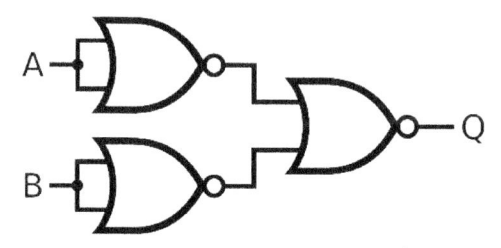

From the table below you can see that the output is only 1 when A and B are both equal to 1. This result is similar to the behavior of an AND Gate. By using only NOR Gates, we were able to reproduce the behavior of the AND Gate. That's why we call the NOR Gate a **Universal Logic Gate**.

A	Input 1st NOR Gate	Output 1st NOR Gate	B	Input 2nd NOR Gate	Output 2nd NOR Gate	Input 3rd NOR Gate	Q
0	00	1	0	00	1	11	0
0	00	1	1	11	0	10	0
1	11	0	0	00	1	01	0
1	11	0	1	11	0	00	1

2) Nancy the NAND Gate

Let's look again at the **Boolean Truth Table** of the NAND Gate:

		A	
		0	1
B	0	1	1
	1	1	0

We are able to reproduce the behavior of the NAND Gate by only using NOR Gates. We can do this in the following way:

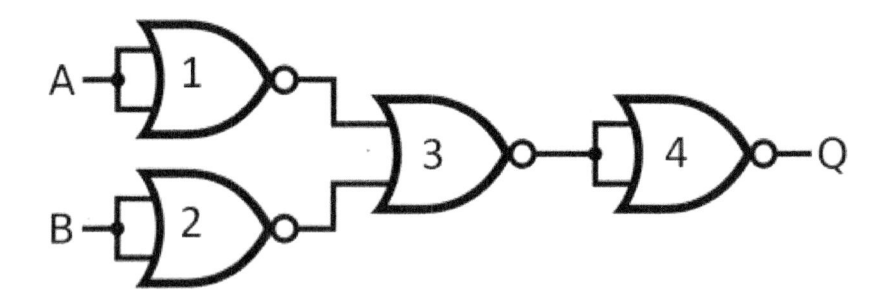

We have four NOR Gates. From the table below you can see that the output is only 0 when A and B are equal to 1. This result is similar to the behavior of an NAND Gate.

A	Input 1st NOR Gate	Output 1st NOR Gate	B	Input 2nd NOR Gate	Output 2nd NOR Gate
0	00	1	0	00	1
0	00	1	1	11	0
1	11	0	0	00	1
1	11	0	1	11	0

Input 3rd NOR Gate	Output 3rd NOR Gate	Input 4th NOR Gate	Q
11	0	00	1
10	0	00	1
01	0	00	1
00	1	11	0

3) Olly and Olliver the OR Gates

Let's look again at the **Boolean Truth Table** of the OR Gate:

		A	
		0	1
B	0	0	1
	1	1	1

We are able to reproduce the behavior of the OR Gate by only using NOR Gates. We can do this in the following way:

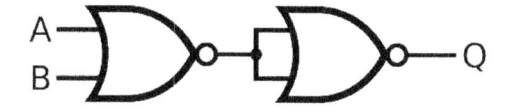

From the table below you can see that the output is only 0 when A and B are equal to 0. This result is similar to the behavior of an OR Gate.

A	B	Output 1st NOR Gate	Input 2nd NOR Gate	Q
0	0	1	11	0
0	1	0	00	1
1	0	0	00	1
1	1	0	00	1

4) Superhero Olly the XOR Gate
Let's look again at the **Boolean Truth Table** of the XOR Gate:

	A	
	0	1
B 0	0	1
B 1	1	0

We are able to reproduce the behavior of the XOR Gate by only using NOR Gates. We can do this in the following way:

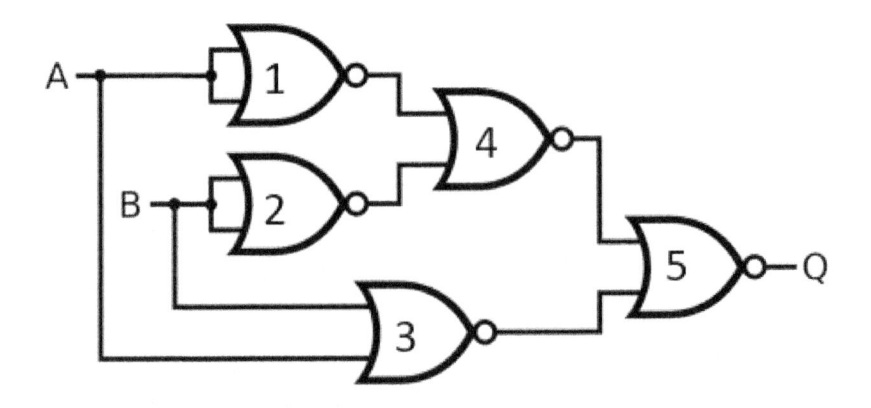

We now have five NOR Gates. From the table below you can see that the output is only 1 when only A or only B is equal to 1. This result is similar to the behavior of an XOR Gate.

A	Input 1st NOR Gate	Output 1st NOR Gate	B	Input 2nd NOR Gate	Output 2nd NOR Gate
0	00	1	0	00	1
0	00	1	1	11	0
1	11	0	0	00	1
1	11	0	1	11	0

Input 3rd NOR Gate	Output 3rd NOR Gate	Input 4th NOR Gate	Output 4th NOR Gate	Input 5th NOR Gate	Q
00	1	11	0	01	0
10	0	10	0	00	1
01	0	01	0	00	1
11	0	00	1	10	0

5) Superhero Nora the XNOR Gate

Let's look again at the **Boolean Truth Table** of the XNOR Gate:

		A	
		0	1
B	0	1	0
	1	0	1

We are able to reproduce the behavior of the XNOR Gate by only using NOR Gates. We can do this in the following way:

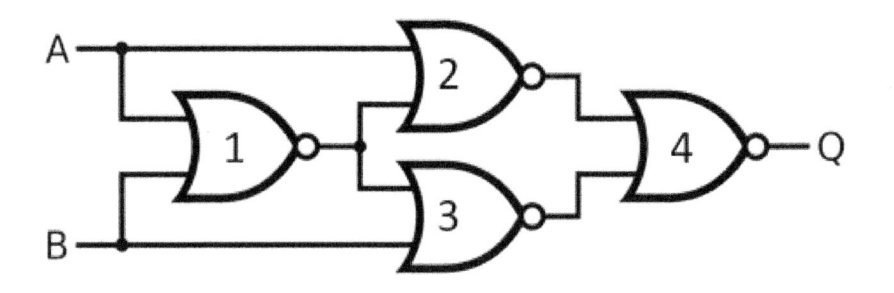

We now have four NOR Gates. From the table below you can see that the output is only 1 when A and B are both equal to 0 or 1. This result is similar to the behavior of an XNOR Gate.

A	B	Input 1st NOR Gate	Output 1st NOR Gate	Input 2nd NOR Gate	Output 2nd NOR Gate
0	0	00	1	01	0
0	1	01	0	00	1
1	0	10	0	10	0
1	1	11	0	10	0

Input 3rd NOR Gate	Output 3rd NOR Gate	Input 4th NOR Gate	Q
10	0	00	1
01	0	10	0
00	1	01	0
01	0	00	1

6) Nellie the NOT Gate

Let's look again at the **Boolean Truth Table** of the NOT Gate:

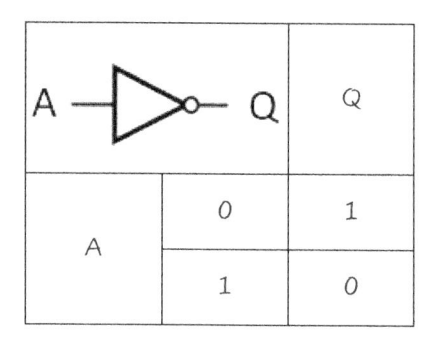

A	Q
0	1
1	0

We are able to reproduce the behavior of the NOT Gate by only using NOR Gates. We can do this in the following way:

This is easy! The final output will be 1 when A is equal to 0. The output is 0 when A is equal to 1. This result is similar to the behavior of a NOT Gate.

A	Input NOR Gate	Q
0	00	1
1	11	0

Wow! We learned how NAND Gates and NOR Gates can be combined to create any other kind of gate. They are **Universal Logic Gates**. It's like magic! A fun thing to know: The smart people who discovered that all the other gates can be created by only NAND Gates or NOR Gates, were Mr. Sheffer and Mr. Peirce. As a tribute, the NAND Gate is sometimes called "Sheffer stroke", while the NOR Gate is sometimes called "Peirce's arrow".

7. Some Strange Creatures

What a journey we've already made! We started learning about our three new friends: Andy the AND Gate, Olly the OR Gate, and Nellie the NOT Gate. We got to know some family members of them: Andrea the AND Gate, Olliver the OR Gate, and Nelson the Buffer. After that, we encountered Nancy the NAND Gate and Nora the NOR Gate. We learned about superpowers as we met XOR and XNOR Gates. Finally, we learned how Universal Logic Gates work.

Now it's time to meet some strange creatures that will all act somewhat special. Don't be afraid. Let's do this!

The IMPLY and NIMPLY Gate

To understand the IMPLY Gate, we immediately look at the **Boolean Truth Table** of this gate:

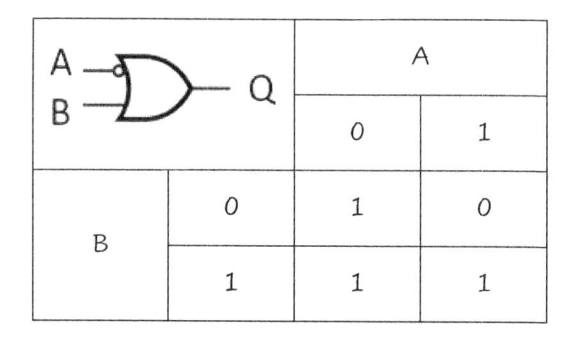

		A	A
		0	1
B	0	1	0
	1	1	1

You notice that the symbol looks similar to that of Olly the OR Gate. However, the IMPLY Gate has a **Bubble** at input A, meaning that this input is turned upside down (1 becomes 0, and 0 becomes 1) before the gate acts as an OR Gate. As a result, the answer will always be 1, unless A is equal to 1 and B is equal to 0. Do you understand why this is the case? When A is equal to 1, the Bubble will change the input to 0. Together with B equal to 0, the output will then be 0.

To understand the NIMPLY Gate, we also look at the **Boolean Truth Table** of this gate:

		A	
		0	1
B	0	0	1
	1	0	0

NIMPLY stands for NOT-IMPLY, meaning that this gate will output the opposite of what the IMPLY Gate will give as result. You see in the table that the answer will only be 1 where the IMPLY Gate answers 0. The answer will be 0 where the IMPLY Gate answers 1.

You notice that the symbol looks similar to that of Andy the AND Gate. However, the NIMPLY Gate has a **Bubble** at input B, meaning that this input is turned upside down (1 becomes 0, and 0 becomes 1) before the gate acts as an AND Gate. As a result, the answer will always be 0, unless A is equal to 1 and B is equal to 0. Do you again understand why this is the case? When B is equal to 0, the Bubble will change the input to 1. Together with A equal to 1, the output will then be 1.

The Tristate Buffer

We learned about Nelson the Buffer, who outputs the same as the input he gets. You remember that his **Boolean Truth Table** looks very simple:

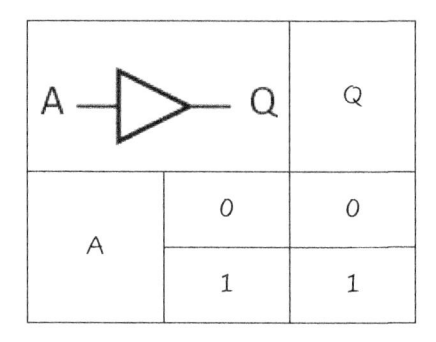

A —▷— Q	Q
A 0	0
1	1

Now imagine that we want to have some mechanism that will act as a switch. When the switch is open, the buffer will not give an output. However, when the switch is closed, the buffer will give an output. How could we create such a mechanism?

A Tristate Buffer will act as the mechanism we are looking for. The word 'Tristate' refers to the fact that the buffer can give three outcomes. While Nelson the Buffer is only capable of answering 0 or 1, the Tristate Buffer can also give no answer when the switch is open. In the **Boolean Truth Table** below, the switch is indicated by input B. If B has the value 1, the switch is closed and the buffer will give the value of A as output. If B has the value 0, the switch is open and the buffer will give no answer.

	B		B
A —▷— Q		0	1
A 0			0
1			1

The Mux and Demux

Imagine we want to have some mechanism that will act as a selector. When we have multiple inputs, the mechanism must select the input we want and further give the selected input as output.

The Mux—sometimes called the Multiplexer—will act as the mechanism we are looking for. The Mux can have multiple inputs from which one is selected and forwarded to the output. The most simple Mux is having two inputs. We call this type a 2-to-1 Mux, as the two inputs are transformed to one output. More complex Muxes can have more inputs, like the 4-to-1, 8-to-1, or 16-to-1 Mux. Below we will explain the 2-to-1 Mux.

Traditionally, a Mux is displayed by a trapezoid. With the long side containing the inputs, and the short side containing the output. A 2-to-1 Mux has two inputs (A and B) and one output (Q). The selection happens by the input S.

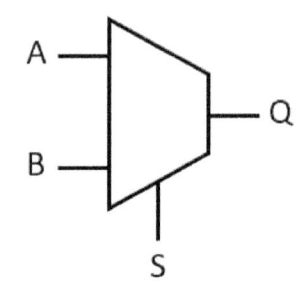

To understand how the 2-to-1 Mux works, we look at the **Boolean Truth Table**. The input S selects the input value we want. When S equals 0, we want the have input A. When S equals 1, we want to have input B. As the selected input is forwarded to the output, Q will equal A when S is 0. Q will equal B when S is 1. Can you figure out how this Mux can be constructed using AND, OR, and NOT Gates?

S	A	B	Q
0	0	0	0
0	0	1	0
0	1	0	1
0	1	1	1
1	0	0	0
1	0	1	1
1	1	0	0
1	1	1	1

To construct a 2-to-1 Mux, we meet out friends Andy, Olly, and Nellie again! We need one NOT Gate, two AND Gates, and one OR Gate. From the table below you can see that the output will equal A when S is 0. The output will equal B when S is 1. This is how the 2-to-1 Mux behaves!

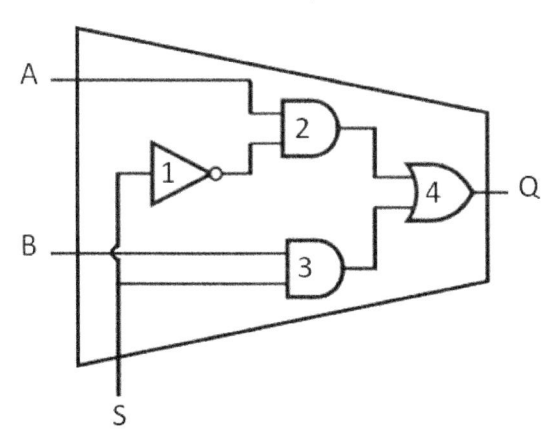

S	Output 1st NOT Gate	A	Input 2nd AND Gate	Output 2nd AND Gate	B	Input 3rd AND Gate
0	1	0	01	0	0	00
0	1	0	01	0	1	10
0	1	1	11	1	0	00
0	1	1	11	1	1	10
1	0	0	00	0	0	01
1	0	0	00	0	1	11
1	0	1	10	0	0	01
1	0	1	10	0	1	11

Output 3rd AND Gate	Input 4th OR Gate	Q
0	00	0
0	00	0
0	10	1
0	10	1
0	00	0
1	01	1
0	00	0
1	01	1

We learned that the Mux can be seen as a selector that picks one of the multiple inputs and passes it through a single output. Now imagine we want to have some mechanism that will do the opposite of what the Mux is doing. When there is only one input and multiple outputs, the mechanism must transmit the input to the selected output.

The Demux—sometimes called the Demultiplexer—will act as the mechanism we are looking for. The Demux has one input which is forwarded to an output that is selected out of multiple outputs. The most simple Demux is having two outputs. We call this type a 1-to-2 Demux, as the single input is transmitted to one out of two selected outputs. More complex Demuxes can have more outputs, like the 1-to-4, 1-to-8, or 1-to-16 Demux. Below we will explain the 1-to-2 Demux.

Similar as the Mux, a Demux is displayed by a trapezoid. With the long side containing the inputs, and the short side containing the output. A 1-to-2 Demux has one input (A) and two outputs (Q1 and Q2). The selection happens by the input S.

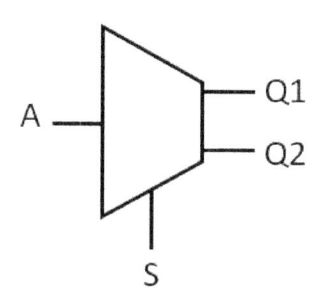

To understand how the 1-to-2 Demux works, we look at the **Boolean Truth Table**. The input S selects the output we want to transmit the input to. When S equals 0, we want to transmit input A to output Q1. When S equals 1, we want to transmit input A to output Q2. Can you figure out how this Demux can be constructed using AND and NOT Gates?

S	A	Q1	Q2
0	0	0	0
0	1	1	0
1	0	0	0
1	1	0	1

To construct a 1-to-2 Demux, we meet out friends Andy and Nellie again! We need one NOT Gate and two AND Gates. From the table below you can see that the output Q1 will equal A when S is 0. The output Q2 will equal A when S is 1. This is how the 1-to-2 Demux behaves!

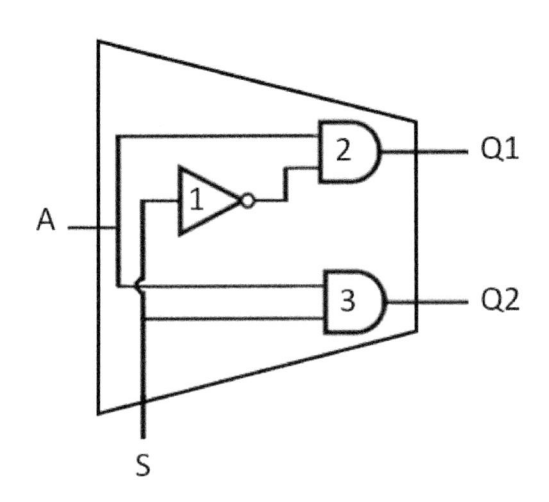

| | Output | | Input | | Input | |
S	1st NOT Gate	A	2nd AND Gate	Q1	3rd AND Gate	Q2
0	1	0	01	0	00	0
0	1	1	11	1	10	0
1	0	0	00	0	01	0
1	0	1	10	0	11	1

Let's make some exercises about these strange creatures. Do you still remember how everything we learned so far works?

Andy & Andrea	AND Gate	
Nancy	NAND Gate	
Olly & Olliver	OR Gate	
Superhero	XOR Gate	

Nora	NOR Gate	A, B → Q
Superhero	XNOR Gate	A, B → Q
Nellie	NOT Gate	A → Q
Nelson	Buffer	A → Q
Strange Creatures	IMPLY Gate	A, B → Q
	NIMPLY Gate	A, B → Q
	Tristate Buffer	A → Q (B control)
	Mux	A, B, S → Q
	Demux	A, S → Q1, Q2

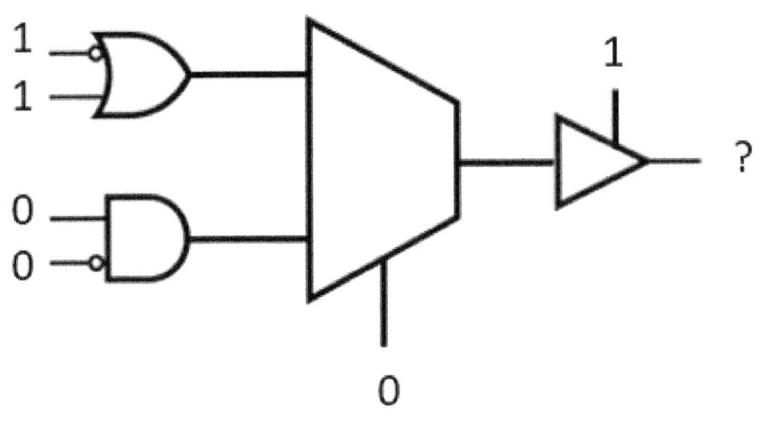

Q 31

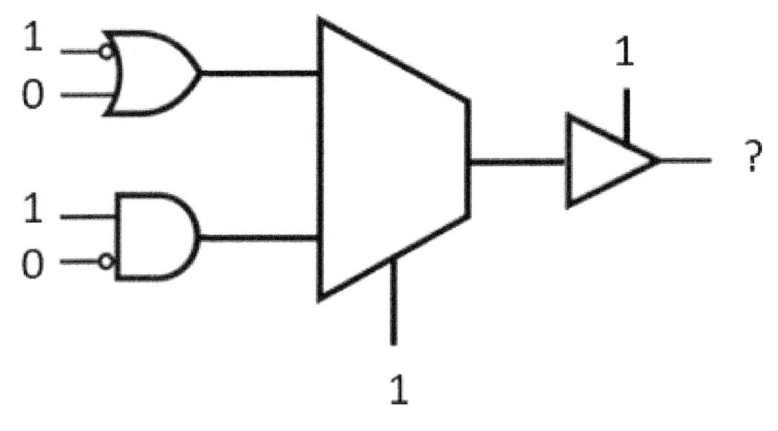

Q 32

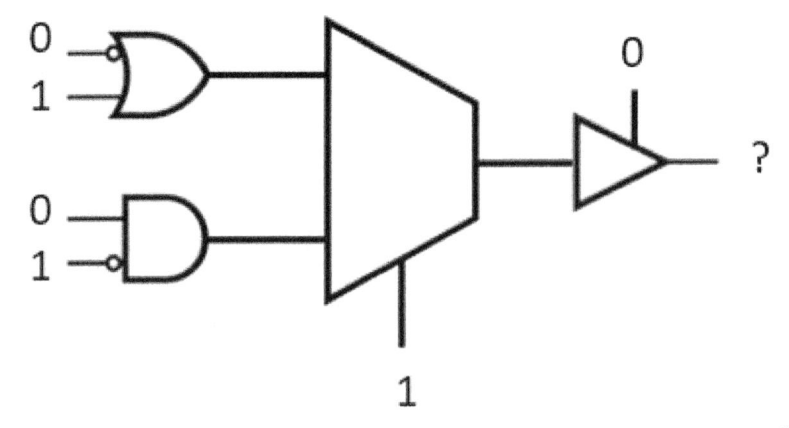

Q 33

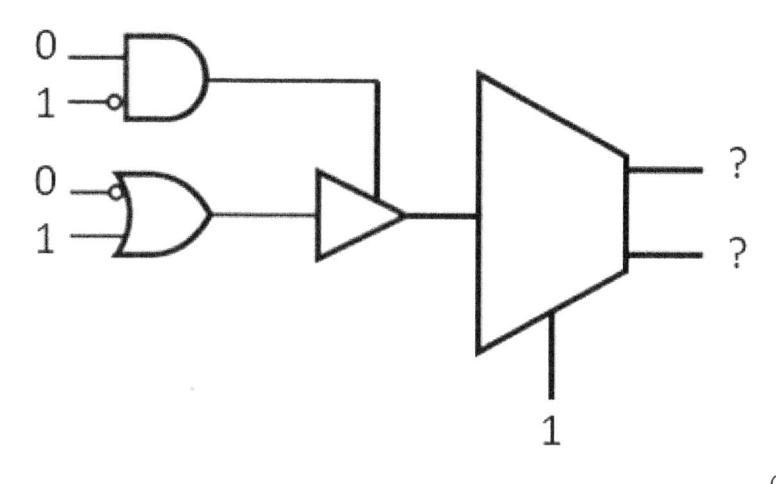

Q 34

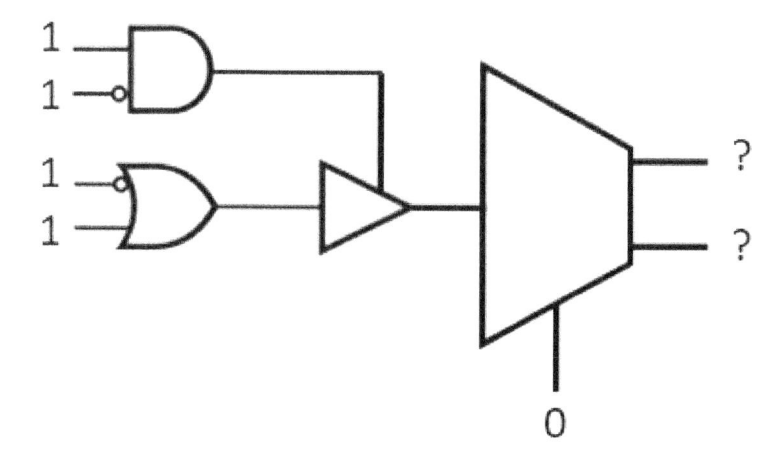

Q 35

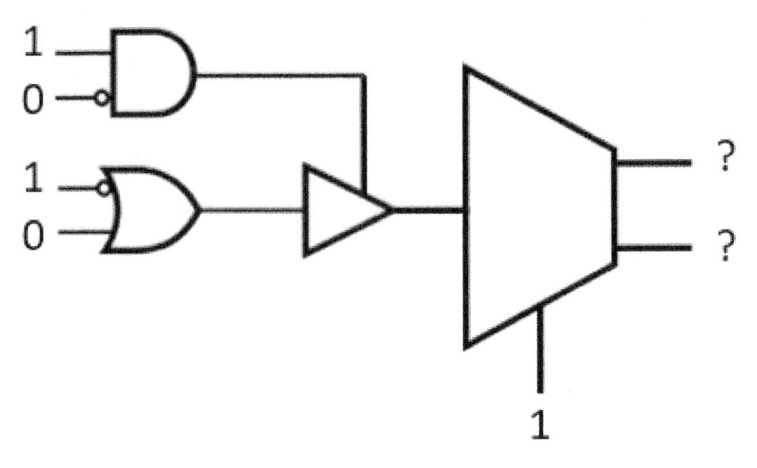

Q 36

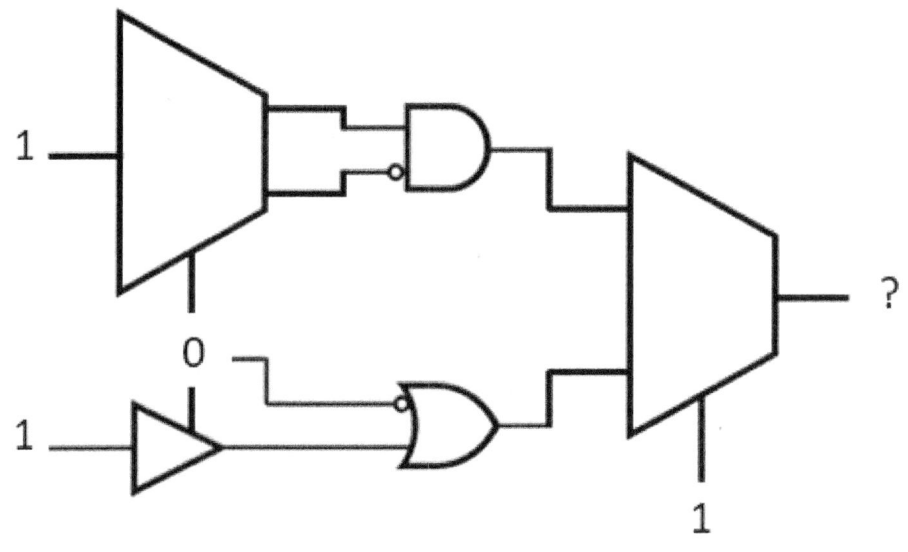

Q 37

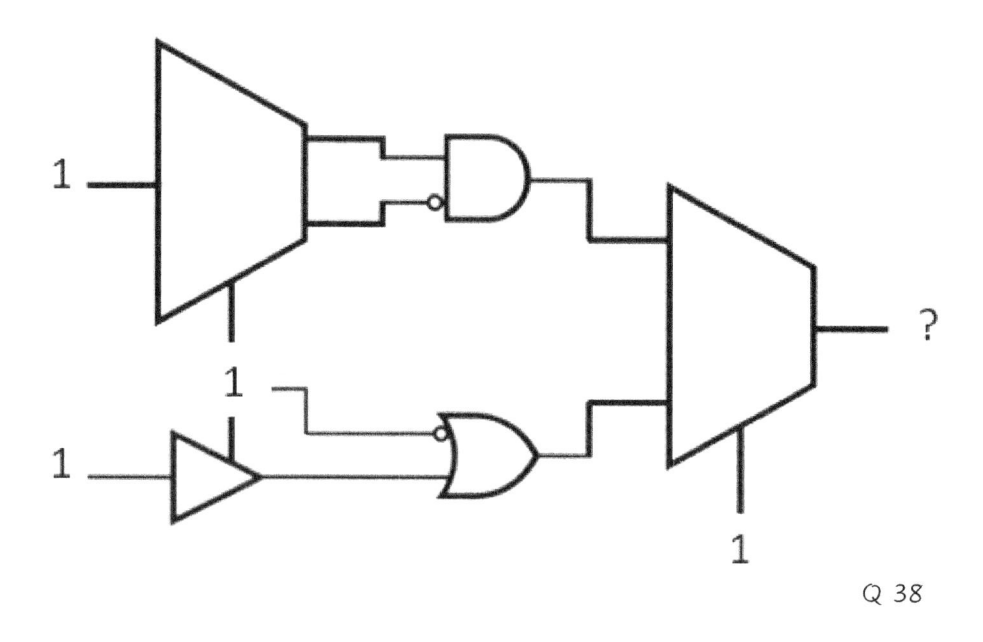

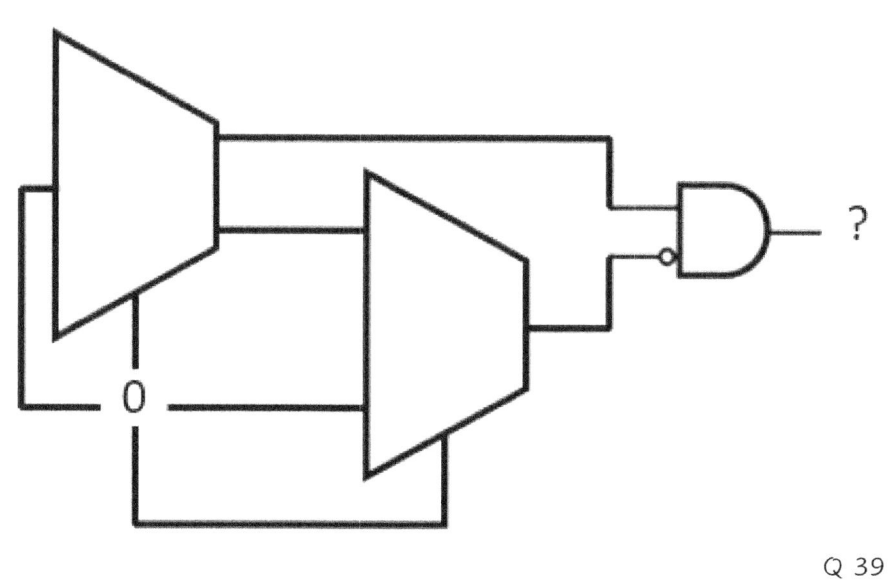

Q 38

Q 39

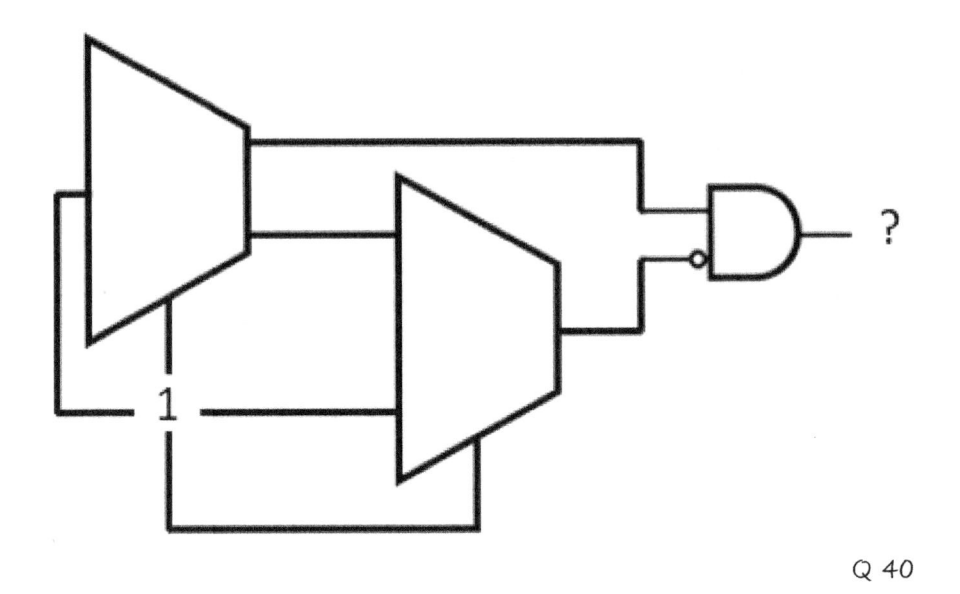

Q 40

8. The Snakes are coming...

One of the most important tasks for a computer is to add binary numbers together. A single binary digit is what we worked with in the previous pages: It can be a 0 or a 1. To add binary digits together, a computer will use an **Adder** for this. Aah, a snake...

No reason to be afraid here! An Adder is not a snake but a device that will perform the addition of binary digits in a correct way. Addition of binary digits is not the same as just adding digits like you are used to do with normal numbers. For example, if we have two times the input 1, adding these binary digits is not equal to 2! Let's first try to understand the wonders of Binary Addition.

Binary Addition
You learned how to add two normal numbers together. When we have two numbers smaller than 10, and the sum is equal or larger than 10, we place an extra 1 before the part of the sum that exceeds 10. Wow, that's a difficult sentence to understand. Let's give an example!

We have two numbers smaller than 10: For example 5 and 7. The sum of these numbers is larger than 10. The part of the sum that exceeds 10 equals 2. So we place an extra 1 before the number 2, which becomes 12 = 5 + 7. Another example to fully understand this: The part of the sum of 5 and 5 that exceeds 10 equals 0. We place a 1 before 0 to get 10 = 5 + 5. This procedure is called Decimal Addition. The extra 1 that is placed before the part of the sum that exceeds 10 is called the **Carry**. The value 10 is called the **Radix** and is equal to 10 as there are ten unique digits that we can use to write numbers within the Decimal world: 0, 1, 2, 3, 4, 5, 6, 7, 8, and 9.

Now assume we want to add a third number smaller than 10 to the sum of the two numbers we just made. If the result of the addition is smaller than two times ten, no new Carry value appears. If the result of the addition is equal or larger than two times ten, a Carry value of 1 appears that is added to the first Carry value: The new Carry value equals 2. This Carry value is placed before the part of the sum that exceeds two times ten. Let's give again an example to understand this!

Our previous sum was equal to 12. We want to add the number 6 to this. As the sum does not exceed two times 10, we just add 6 to 12, which becomes 18. If we want to add the number 9 to the sum of 12, the result becomes larger than two times ten. We will then have an extra Carry of 1 that is added to the first Carry. The new Carry becomes 2, which is placed before the part of the sum that exceeds two times ten. The final sum becomes 21 = 12 + 9.

Within Binary Addition a somewhat similar procedure is followed. We start with two single binary digits which can both be 0 or 1. The Carry is equal to 1. The Radix equals the number of unique digits that exist in the binary world. This equals 2, as we can only use a 0 or a 1. The procedure then becomes: When we have two numbers and the sum is equal or larger than 2, we place an extra 1 before the part of the sum that exceeds 2. An example is needed here!

We have two single binary digits: 1 and 1. The sum of these digits is equal to 2. We thus place an extra 1 before the part of the sum that exceeds 2. This becomes: 10. The result is now not the number ten, but the binary number 10, read as 'one zero':

```
          1
  +       1
  ─────────────
          1        = Carry
         1 0
```

In a general way, we can write the Binary Addition we just made also in the following way. This will be helpful when we learn how the Half Adder works:

```
         A
+        B
   ─────────
         C        = Carry
   ─────────
         C  S
```

Assume we want to add together two binary numbers that each contain two digits. For example, we want to add the binary numbers 11 and 11 together. The procedure remains the same: Each time the sum of the digits that are underneath each other is equal or larger than 2, a Carry of 1 is created. This Carry is placed underneath the digits one place to the left. Adding 11 and 11 together results in the binary outcome of 110:

```
         1  1
+        1  1
   ─────────────
      1  1          = Carry
   ─────────────
      1  1  0
```

In a general way, we can write the Binary Addition we just made also in the following way. This will be helpful when we learn how the Full Adder works:

```
         A2  A1
+        B2  B1
   ───────────────
      C3  C2        = Carry
   ───────────────
      S3  S2  S1
```

Luckily, we don't have to make all the calculations ourselves when we want to add binary digits. A computer will use an Adder for this. We can make a distinction between a Half Adder and a Full Adder. Let's learn how this works!

The Half Adder

The Half Adder will add two single binary digits together in a correct way. It has two inputs (A and B), and the Carry (C) and Sum (S) of the addition as output.

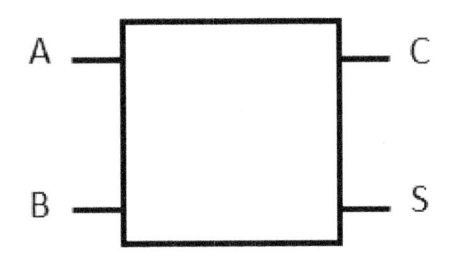

```
A ─┤    ├─ C
   │    │
B ─┤    ├─ S
```

As we already know how Binary Addition works, we know we can expect the following **Boolean Truth Table** of the Half Adder:

A	B	C	S
0	0	0	0
0	1	0	1
1	0	0	1
1	1	1	0

We learned that adding the single binary digits 1 and 1 together, the result is the binary number 10. The first digit of this number (1) is given by the Carry, the second digit (0) is represented by the Sum output. Can you figure out how the Half Adder can be constructed using AND and XOR Gates?

To construct a Half Adder, we meet out friends Andy and superhero Olly again! We need one AND Gate and one XOR Gate. If you go through the logic of each gate, you see that the output of the Sum and the Carry is similar to the output of the Half Adder. When adding the single binary digits 1 and 1 together, the exclusive property of the XOR Gate will result in a Sum of 0. The AND Gate gets two times a 1 as input and will make the Carry equal to 1!

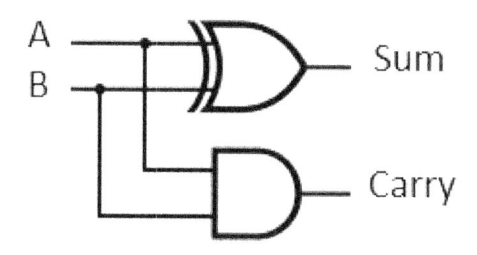

Remark that in the figure above, we used something we did not use before: black dots at the intersection of lines. From now on these black dots represent that the two lines touch each other and that an input is forwarded into the two lines. When lines that touch each other in the scheme don't have a black dot on the intersection, then these lines are NOT touching each other! Don't forget this!

The Full Adder
The Full Adder will add two single binary digits and a Carry value from a previous addition together in a correct way. For example, if you look back at the sum we made on the previous page, when we want to add A2, B2, and C2 together, we can not use a Half Adder as we now have three digits to add together. C2 is the Carry value from a previous addition. The Full Adder is able to add three digits together in a correct way. It has three inputs: A and B as the single binary digits, and Cin which represents the Carry value from a previous addition. The output is Cout which represents an output Carry value and the Sum S of the addition.

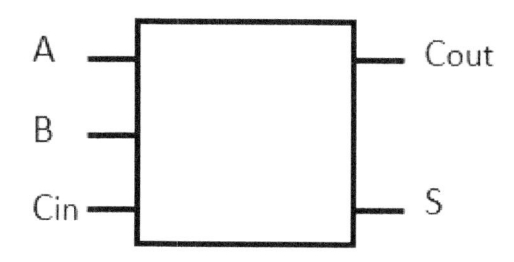

You are an expert in Binary Addition by now, so you know we can expect the following **Boolean Truth Table** of the Full Adder:

A	B	Cin	Cout	S
0	0	0	0	0
0	0	1	0	1
0	1	0	0	1
0	1	1	1	0
1	0	0	0	1
1	0	1	1	0
1	1	0	1	0
1	1	1	1	1

Looking back at the sum we made before, adding A2, B2, and C2 together corresponds with the last row of the table. The Carry value created by the addition (C3) is given by the output Cout. The sum of the addition (S2) is given by the output S. Can you figure out how the Full Adder can be constructed using AND, OR and XOR Gates?

To construct a Full Adder, we meet out friends Andy, Olly, and superhero Olly again! We need two AND Gates, two XOR Gates, and one OR Gate. By now, you should be able to go through the logic of each gate and to see that the output of the Sum and the output Carry is similar to the output of the Full Adder.

When adding the single binary digits 1 and 1 together, combined with an input Carry of 1, the exclusive property of the two XOR Gates will result in a Sum of 1. The combination of two AND Gates followed by an OR Gate will make the output Carry equal to 1!

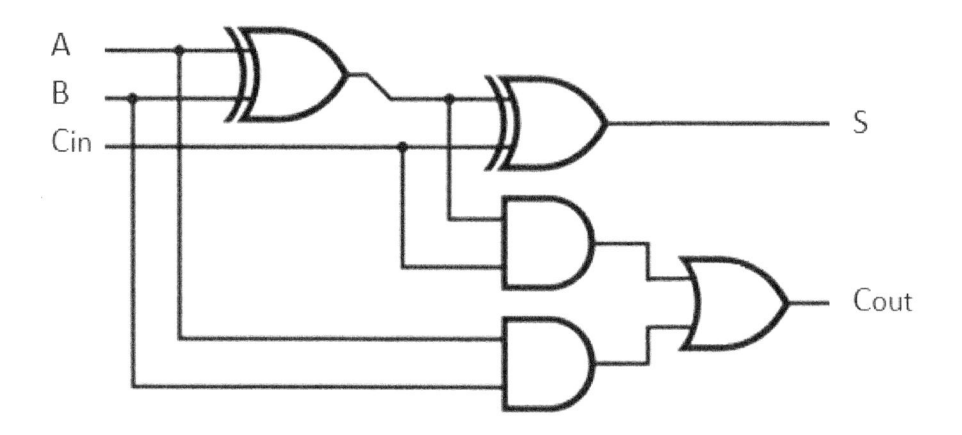

In practice, a Half Adder and Full Adder are mostly combined in a sequence to make complex additions possible. For example, think back at the sum we made before in which we added the binary numbers 11 and 11 together:

```
        1   1                         A2   A1
  +     1   1                  +      B2   B1
       ─────────                     ──────────
        1   1     = Carry =      C3   C2
       ─────────                     ──────────
    1   1   0                    S3   S2   S1
```

To make this addition, we can not use a Half Adder or Full Adder by itself. The solution is to put the two types of Adders after each other! The Carry output of the Half Adder will become the input Carry of the Full Adder. The final result of the addition is given by the output S1 and S2, combined with the output Carry C3:

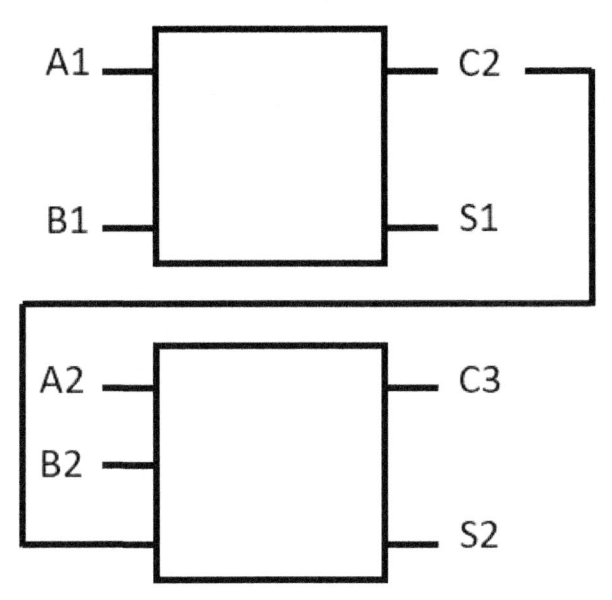

You're becoming an expert in Logic Gated! Are you able to complete the **Boolean Truth Table** of the Half Adder combined with the Full Adder?

A1	B1	C2	A2	B2	C3	S2	S1
0	0	0	0	0	0	0	0
0	0	0	0	1	0	1	0
0	0	0	1	0	0	1	0
0	0	0	1	1	1	0	0
0	1	0	0	0	0	0	1
0	1	0	0	1	0	1	1
0	1	0	1	0	0	1	1
0	1	0	1	1	1	0	1
1	0	0	0	0	0	0	1
1	0	0	0	1	0	1	1
1	0	0	1	0	0	1	1
1	0	0	1	1	1	0	1
1	1	1	0	0	0	1	0
1	1	1	0	1	1	0	0
1	1	1	1	0	1	0	0
1	1	1	1	1	1	1	0

Q 41

9. Something more difficult to end

Until now we always worked with inputs and outputs. The inputs went into one or more logic gates, which resulted into one or more output values.

Now assume we want to have a device that allows us to store data. For example, when we have an input equal to 1, we want to store that value in a certain way as output value. How could we build such a device?

Clever people already thought about this! For example, we can bring Olly the OR Gate back to front in the following way:

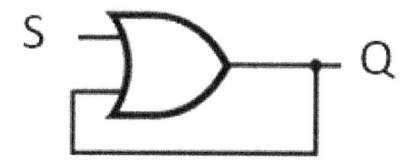

We now only have one input S and an output Q. The output of the gate is also the second input of the gate. We call this output to input connection a **feedback** loop. This already looks somewhat difficult... You learned how the **Boolean Truth Table** of a simple OR Gate works. However, we now have a feedback loop that makes everything more complex. Let's learn how it works!

Assume, we start with nothing. S will be equal to 0. The second input equals 0, making the output Q also 0. Simple as that. When we make S equal to 1 (Step 1), both the second input of the gate and the output Q will become 1. Still easy to understand, right?! Now watch what happens if we switch S again to 0 (Step 2).

The second input of the gate remains equal to 1, which makes the output Q equal to 1. Switching S from 1 to 0 will have no effect on the output Q! Even if we put S again equal to 1 (Step 3), nothing will change: the output Q remains equal to 1! It is like we stored the value 1 in the output Q. We can say "once the input is equal to 1, the output stays equal to 1, it latches on".

	S	Second Input	Q
Start	0	0	0
Step 1	1	1	1
Step 2	0	1	1
Step 3	1	1	1

So how could we be able to switch the output back to 0? This turns out to be impossible when we only use an OR Gate with a feedback loop. We need something even more complex.

The complex drawing below is called a **Set–Reset Latch**. We will learn what this means. The input S stands for Set, and the input R stands for Reset. The two outputs are output Q and output $\bar{Q}$, pronounced Qbar, which will always be the opposite value of Q. You remember Nora the NOR Gate? We meet her again here, two times! We point to them as the Upper NOR Gate and Down NOR Gate. Let's try to understand this difficult creature!

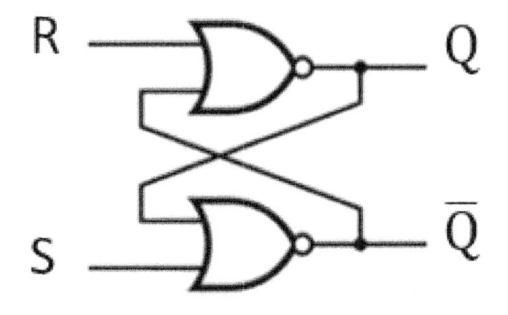

Assume, we start with nothing: R and S equal to 0 and assume the second input of the upper NOR Gate equals 0. If you go through the logic of the NOR Gates, you will see that the output Q will equal 1 and Qbar equals 0. This should not be too hard to see, right?! When we change S to 1, nothing will change to the outputs. We can say "By making S equal to 1, we set the output Q equal to 1". Now watch what happens if we switch R again to 1 while S equals 0 (Step 2). First, the input of the upper NOR Gate equals 1 and 0, giving 0 as output. The input of the down NOR Gate will as a result equal 0 and 0 with 1 as an output. As this output feedbacks to the upper NOR Gate, the inputs are in a second step changed to 1 and 1, resulting in a 0 as output. The final result is that Q equals 0 and Qbar equals 1. By switching R from 0 to 1, we switched the values of the outputs! We can say "By making R equal to 1, we reset the output Q back to 0". If we put R back equal to 0 (Step 3) we end up with the opposite output as the start, but with similar values for R and S! Making R again equal to 1 (Step 4) will have no effect on the output. Making S equal to 1 (Step 5) will finally switch the output values again to 1 and 0.

	R	S	Input UPPER NOR	Output UPPER NOR	Input DOWN NOR	Output DOWN NOR	Q	$\bar{Q}$
Start	0	0	00	1	10	0	1	0
Step 1	0	1	00	1	11	0	1	0
Step 2	1	0						
First:			10	0	00	1		
Second:			11	0	00	1	0	1
Step 3	0	0	01	0	00	1	0	1
Step 4	1	0	11	0	00	1	0	1
Step 5	0	1						
First:			01	0	01	0		
Second:			00	1	11	0	1	0

In the table on the previous page, you clearly see how Q and Qbar are always opposite values. Do you already understand why we call this a Set–Reset Latch?

Let's look at the table again with some columns and rows removed. S is called a Set input because by giving it a value of 1, the output Q it set equal to 1 (Step 1). R is called a Reset input because by giving it a value of 1, the output Q is changed to 0 (Step 2). By making S again equal to 1, we set the output back to 1 (Step 5).

	R	S	Q
Start	0	0	1
Step 1	0	1	1
Step 2	1	0	0
Step 3	0	0	0
Step 4	1	0	0
Step 5	0	1	1

The Set–Reset Latch is sometimes displayed as a box with the inputs R and S on the left, and outputs Q and Qbar on the right.

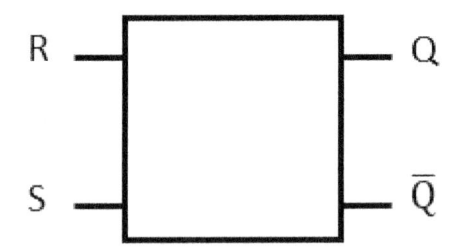

Can you figure out what will happen when we make R and S both equal to 1? Some people call this an invalid state meaning that you are not supposed to do this... But you can try to solve this question anyway, it shouldn't be that difficult.

Q 42

You now fully understand how the Set-Reset Latch works. It is a device that allows us to store data until we reset the device. If you think about it, it is still somewhat inconvenient to have two inputs to set and reset the device. Isn't it possible to create a device that does the same thing but with only one input? This looks very difficult! Luckily some smart people already thought about this. Let's learn how to do this!

The first thing to do is to bring our friend Andy the AND Gate back in action! We need him two times and add them to the Set-Reset Latch in the following way:

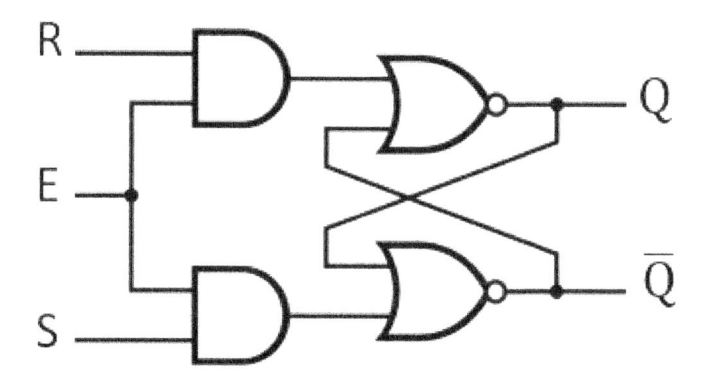

You recognize the Set-Reset Latch at the right side with the outputs Q and Qbar. The inputs R and S are now connected to an AND Gate together with the new input E. We call this input the **Enable** input. When working with an extra input E we have a way to turn the Set-Reset Latch on and off. It is only when E has the value 1 that the other inputs R and S can pass through the Set-Reset Latch. You can think about input E as a gatekeeper. That's why we call this construction a **Gated Set-Reset Latch**.

We now have three inputs, while we want a device with only one input! How can we reach that goal?

We need our friend Nellie the NOT Gate again and place her in front of the Gated Set-Reset Latch in the following way:

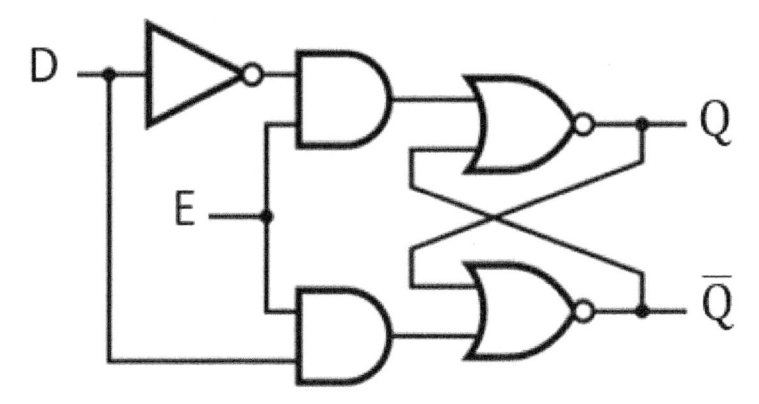

You recognize again the outputs Q and Qbar at the right. We still have the input E. However, the inputs R and S are now replaced by one single input D. We call this device a **D Latch**. The D stands for Data. It works as a Set-Reset Latch that stores the value of the input D. When the Latch is enabled (E = 1), we can set the output Q equal to 1 by putting D equal to 1. When D equals 0, we reset the output Q to 0. In this way, the value of D is stored in the output Q. When the Latch is disabled (E = 0), changing the value of D will have no effect on the output values. The stored value will not be affected. The D Latch is sometimes displayed as a box with the inputs D and E on the left, and outputs Q and Qbar on the right.

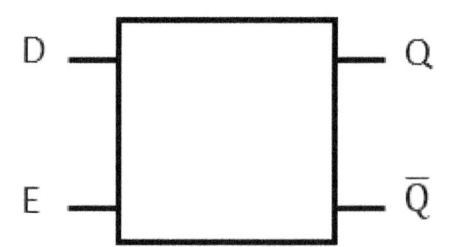

Assume the current values of Q and Qbar are respectively 1 and 0. Can you figure out the **Boolean Truth Table** of the D Latch?

Q 43

Solutions

Q 1:

```
0 ─┐
   ├AND─ 0
1 ─┘
```

An AND Gate only gives 1 as outcome when BOTH inputs are 1. Here, we have 0 and 1 as input, so the output is 0.

Q 2:

A	B	Q
1	0	1
1	1	1
0	0	0
0	1	1

An OR Gate gives 1 as output when at least one of both inputs is 1. Only is line three, we have 0 and 0 as input, so the output is only 0 in line three.

Q 3:

```
0 ─AND─ 0    1 ─AND─ 1    0 ─AND─ 0
0             1             1

0 ─OR─ 0     1 ─OR─ 1     0 ─OR─ 1
0             1             1
```

The difference lies in the third column: An AND Gate only gives 1 as outcome when BOTH inputs are 1. Here, we have 0 and 1 as input, so the output is 0. An OR Gate gives 1 as output when at least one of both inputs is 1. Here, we have 0 and 1 as input, so the output is 1.

Q 4:

We start with the outcome of Olly and write this in each cell in the table. We only get a 0 in the first column as Olly answers "Yes" (1) as long as one of the inputs (A & B) are true:

		AB			
		00	01	10	11
C	0	0	1	1	1
	1	0	1	1	1

Now we add the outcome of Nellie in each cell. Nellie will just answer the opposite of the input (C). So, 0 becomes 1, and 1 becomes 0:

		AB			
		00	01	10	11
C	0	01	11	11	11
	1	00	10	10	10

Now we use the numbers in each cell as the input for Andy. He will answer "Yes" (1) when both Olly and Nellie come up with "Yes" (1) as an answer. So only when there is 11 in a cell, Andy will give 1 as answer:

		AB			
		00	01	10	11
C	0	0	1	1	1
	1	0	0	0	0

82

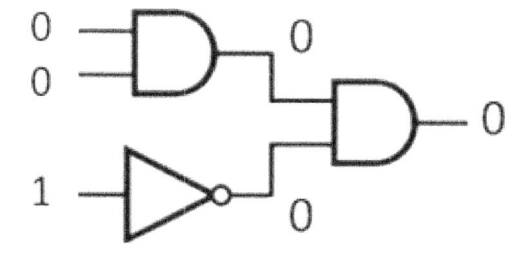

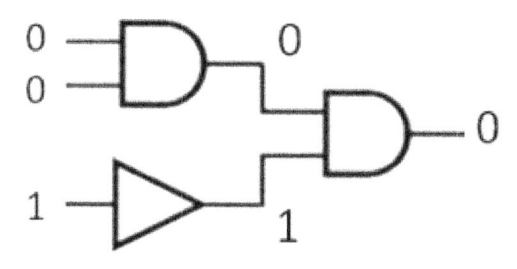

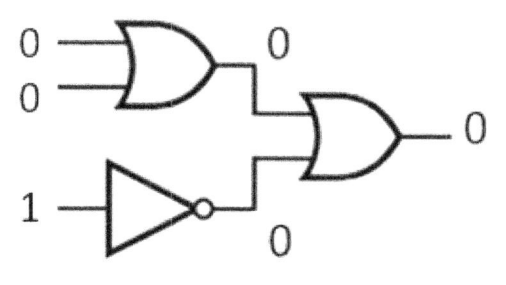

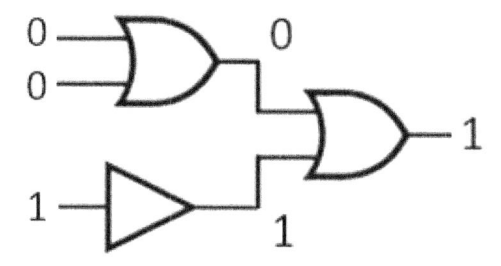

Q 5:

Q 6:

Q 7:

Q 8:

Q 9:

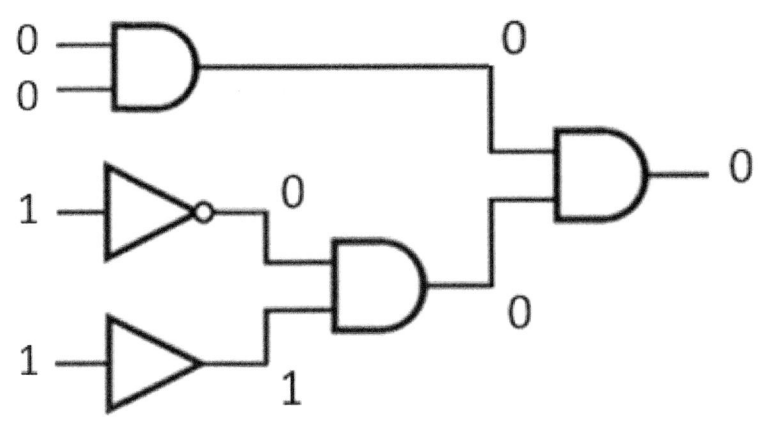

Q 10:

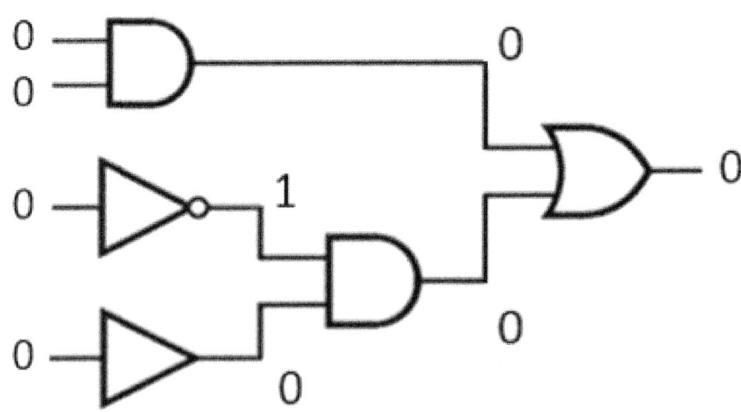

Q 11:

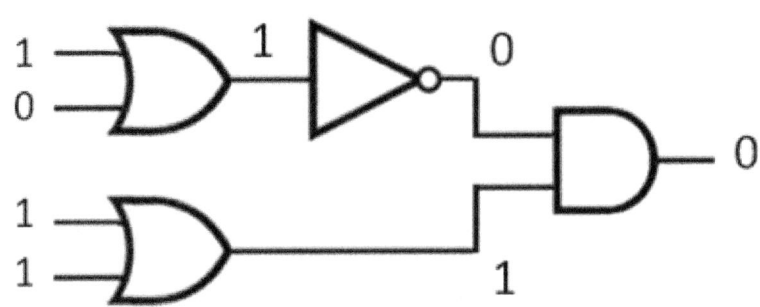

Q 12:

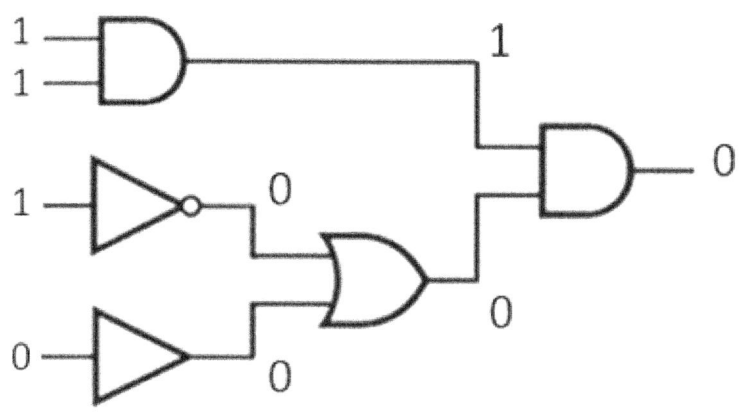

Q 13:

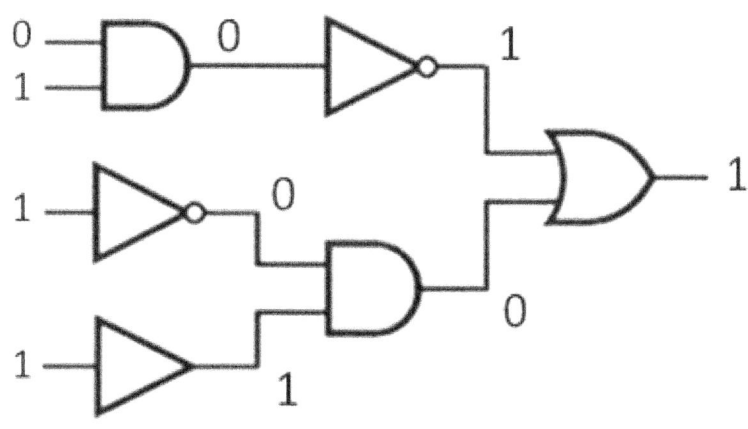

Q 14:

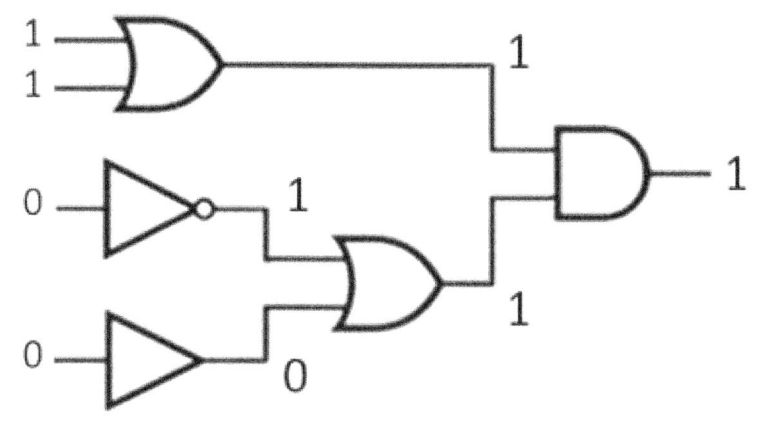

Q 15:

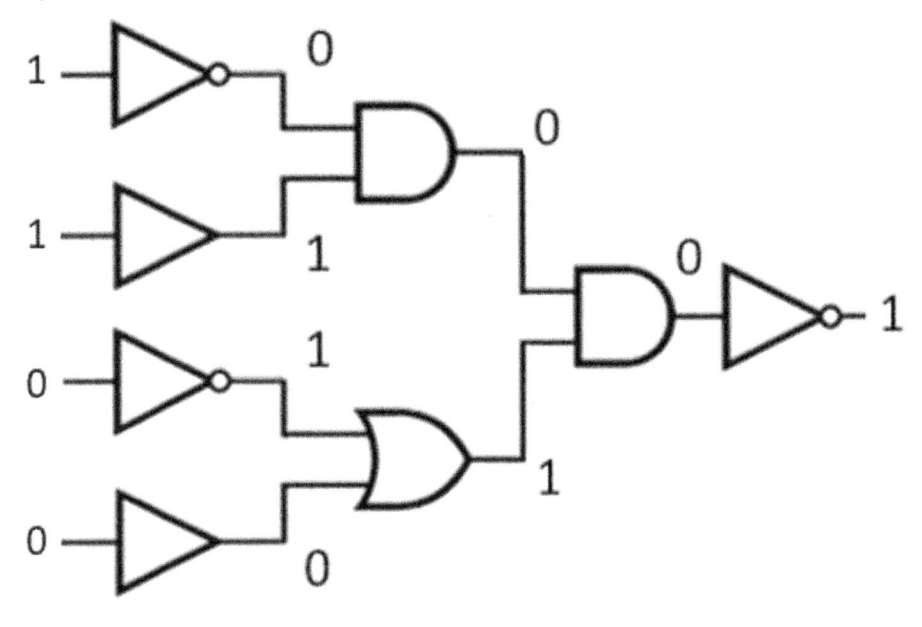

Q 16:

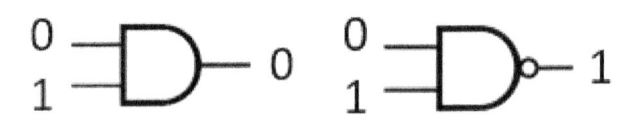

An AND Gate only gives 1 as outcome when BOTH inputs are 1. Here, we have 0 and 1 as input, so the output is 0.
A NAND Gate only gives 1 as outcome, when no or only one input is 1. Here, we have 0 and 1 as input, so the output is 1. The output of the NAND Gate is the opposite of the output of the AND Gate.

Q 17:

```
0 ⟩D⟩ 0      1 ⟩D⟩ 1      0 ⟩D⟩ 1
0              1              1

0 ⟩D⟩o 1     1 ⟩D⟩o 0     0 ⟩D⟩o 0
0              1              1
```

An OR Gate only gives 1 as outcome when at least one of the inputs is true. A NOR Gate only gives 1 as outcome, when no input is true. The output of the NOR Gate is the opposite of the output of the OR Gate.

Q 18:

		AB			
		00	01	10	11
	00	0	1	1	1
CD	01	0	1	1	1
	10	0	1	1	1
	11	1	0	0	0

Q 19:

		AB			
		00	01	10	11
CD	00	1	1	1	1
	01	0	0	0	1
	10	0	0	0	1
	11	0	0	0	1

Q 20:

		AB			
		00	01	10	11
CD	00	0	0	0	0
	01	0	1	1	1
	10	0	1	1	1
	11	0	0	0	0

Q 21:

		AB			
		00	01	10	11
CD	00	1	1	1	1
	01	1	1	1	1
	10	1	1	1	1
	11	1	0	0	0

Q 22:

		AB			
		00	01	10	11
CD	00	0	0	0	1
	01	0	0	0	1
	10	0	0	0	1
	11	0	0	0	0

Q 23:

		AB			
		00	01	10	11
CD	00	1	0	0	0
	01	0	0	0	0
	10	0	0	0	0
	11	1	0	0	0

Q 24:

		AB			
		00	01	10	11
CD	00	1	0	0	0
	01	1	0	0	0
	10	1	0	0	0
	11	0	1	1	1

Q 25:

		AB			
		00	01	10	11
CD	00	0	1	1	1
	01	1	1	1	1
	10	1	1	1	1
	11	0	1	1	1

Q 26:

		AB			
		00	01	10	11
CD	00	1	0	0	0
	01	0	1	1	1
	10	0	1	1	1
	11	1	0	0	0

Q 27:

		AB			
		00	01	10	11
CD	00	0	0	0	1
	01	1	1	1	0
	10	1	1	1	0
	11	0	0	0	1

Q 28:

		AB			
		00	01	10	11
CD	00	1	0	0	1
	01	0	1	1	0
	10	0	1	1	0
	11	1	0	0	1

Q 29:

		AB			
		00	01	10	11
CD	00	0	0	0	1
	01	1	1	1	1
	10	1	1	1	1
	11	0	0	0	1

Q 30:

		AB			
		00	01	10	11
CD	00	0	0	0	1
	01	0	0	0	1
	10	0	0	0	1
	11	1	1	1	1

Q 31:

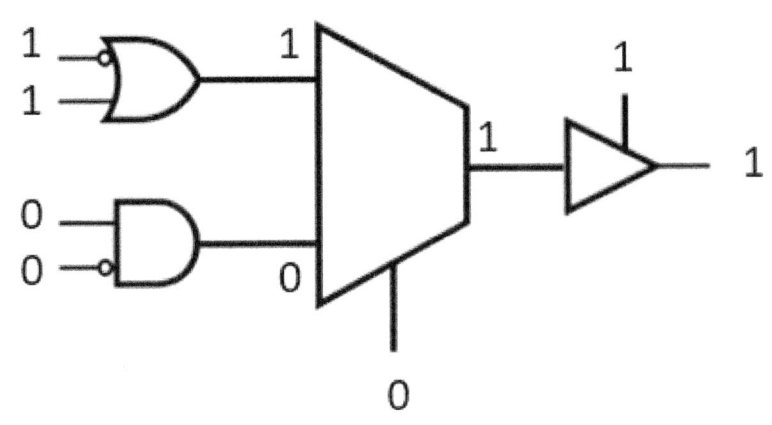

Q 32:

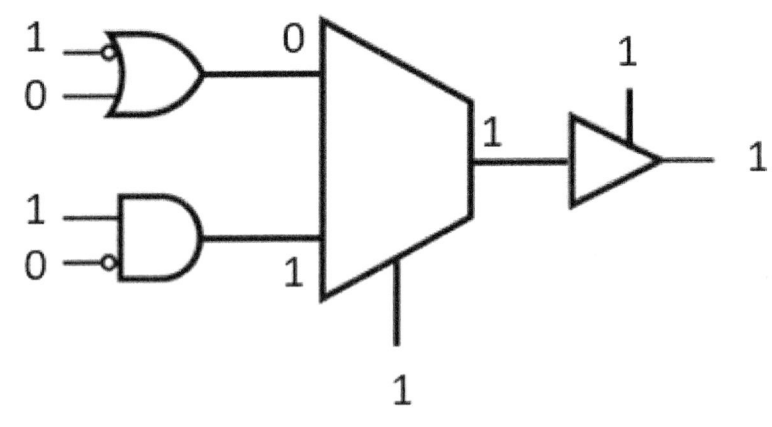

Q 33:

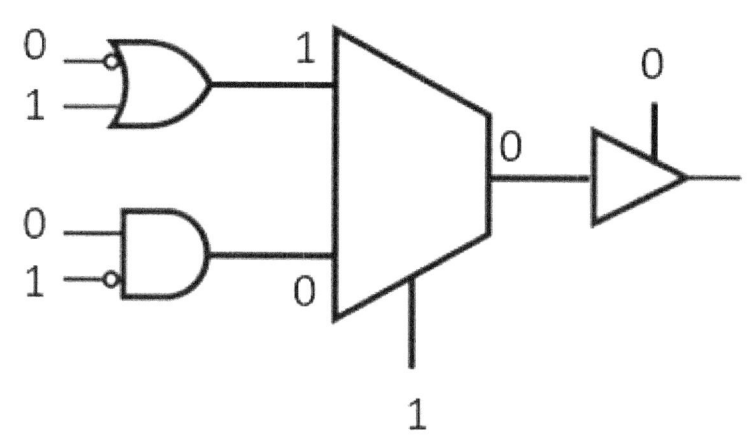

Q 34:

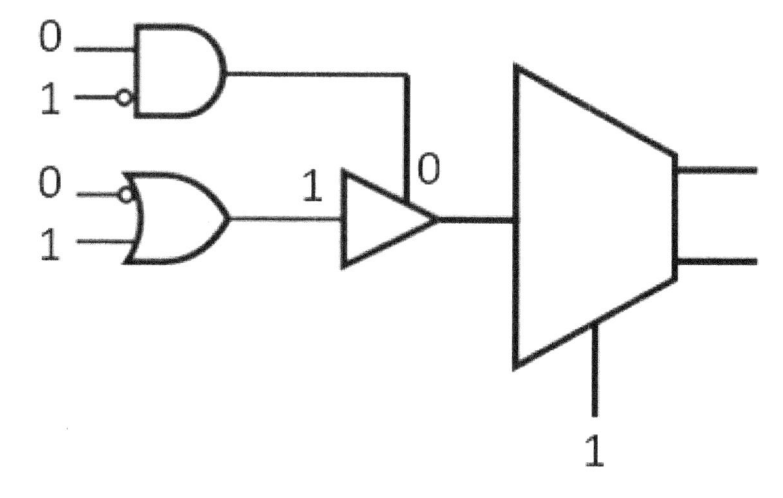

Q 35:

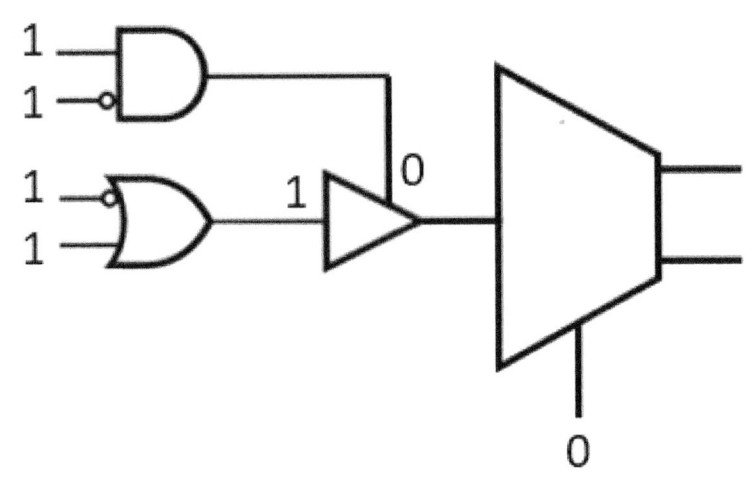

```
1 ─┐
1 ─○┘ ─┐
        │ 0
1 ─○┐ 1  ▷── ┐
1 ─┘       ──┤MUX├──
              │   │
              0
```

Q 36:

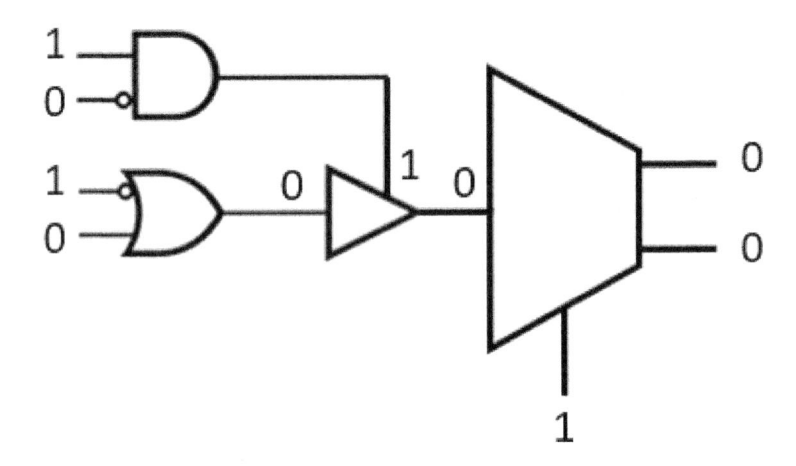

```
1 ─┐
0 ─○┘ ─┐
        │ 1   0
1 ─○┐ 0  ▷──       ── 0
0 ─┘       ──┤MUX├── 0
              │
              1
```

Q 37:

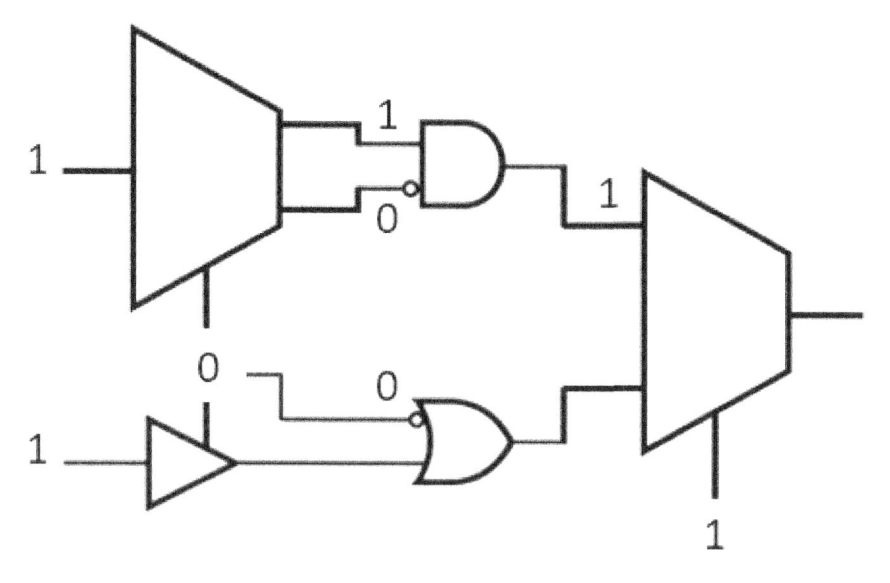

Q 38:

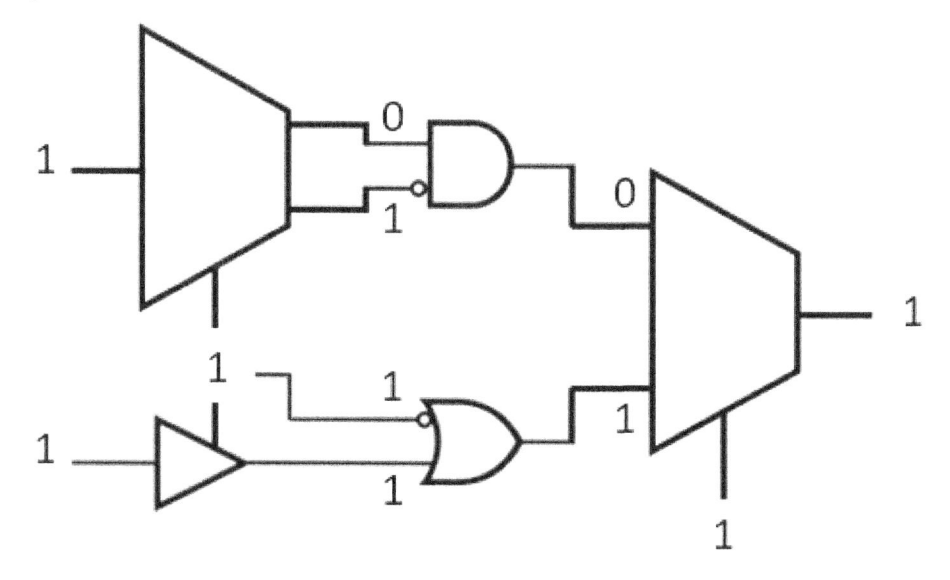

Q 39:

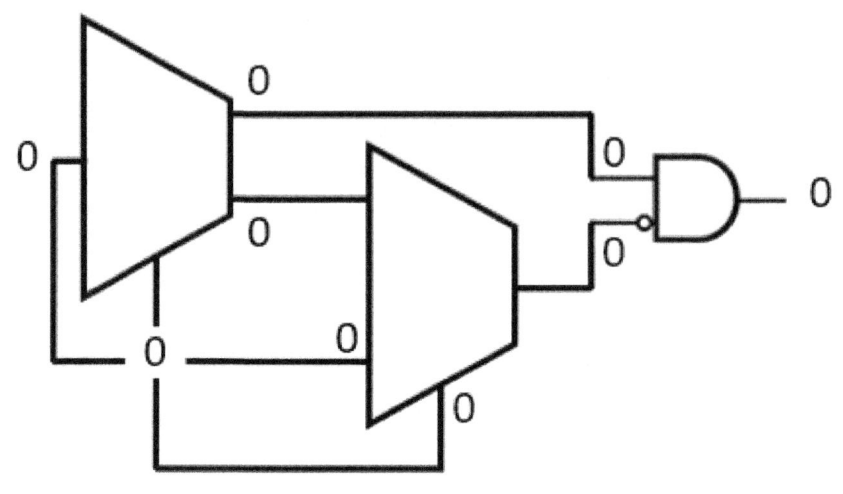

Q 40:

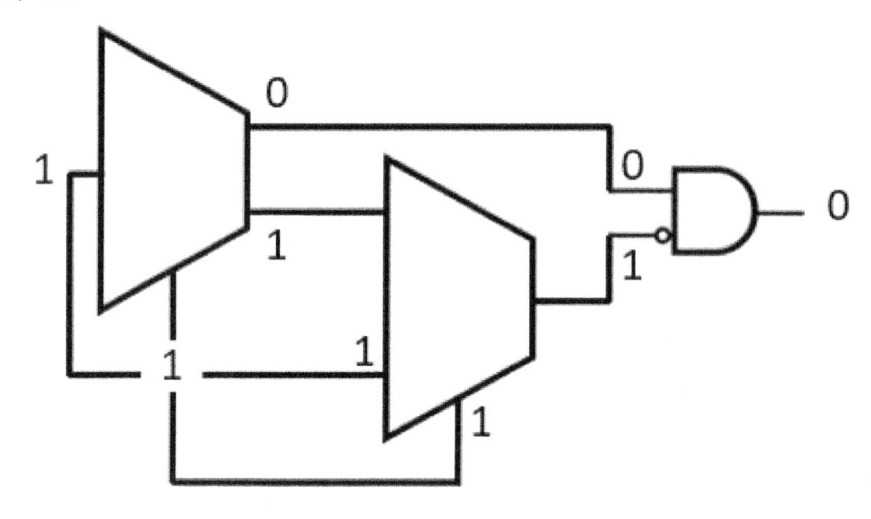

Q 41:

A1	B1	C2	A2	B2	C3	S2	S1
0	0	0	0	0	0	0	0
0	0	0	0	1	0	1	0
0	0	0	1	0	0	1	0
0	0	0	1	1	1	0	0
0	1	0	0	0	0	0	1
0	1	0	0	1	0	1	1
0	1	0	1	0	0	1	1
0	1	0	1	1	1	0	1
1	0	0	0	0	0	0	1
1	0	0	0	1	0	1	1
1	0	0	1	0	0	1	1
1	0	0	1	1	1	0	1
1	1	1	0	0	0	1	0
1	1	1	0	1	1	0	0
1	1	1	1	0	1	0	0
1	1	1	1	1	1	1	0

Q 42:

	R	S	Input UPPER NOR	Output UPPER NOR	Input DOWN NOR	Output DOWN NOR	Q	$\bar{Q}$
Start	0	0	00	1	10	0	1	0
Step 1	0	1	00	1	11	0	1	0
Step 2	1	0						
First:			10	0	00	1		
Second:			11	0	00	1	0	1
Step 3	0	0	01	0	00	1	0	1
Step 4	1	0	11	0	00	1	0	1
Step 5	0	1						
First:			01	0	01	0		
Second:			00	1	11	0	1	0
Step 6	1	1	10	0	01	0	0	0

Q 43:

E	D	Q	$\bar{Q}$
0	0	1	0
0	1	1	0
1	0	0	1
1	1	1	0

You're closer to becoming an expert in Logic Gates now. There is however still more to learn, check the Internet and other books. Goodbye for now!
The end ☹